Ak Tash
Benderski P.
PAMIR
Wakh-jir P
TAGH-DUM-B
PAMIR
Mintaka P.
Wakh-jir R.
Khunjerab R.
Khunjerab P.
Irshad R.
Ashkoman R.
H U N Z A
Hunza
Nilt
Nagar
Rakaposhi
25550
Rakaposhi
Gakuch
Gilgit R.
Shimshal P.
Gilgit
4890
Bunji
Ronda
INDUS R.
Chilas
Astore
Nanga Parbat
26620
Skardo
Burzil P
Shardi
Gurais
Bandipur
K S M I
Wular L
Sopur
Jhelum R.
SRINAGAR

Jimmie Stewart — Frontiersman

The Edited Memoirs of
Major General Sir J.M. Stewart, KCB CMG

Jimmie Stewart — Frontiersman

The Edited Memoirs of
Major General Sir J. M. Stewart, KCB CMG

by

Robert Maxwell

The Pentland Press Ltd.
Edinburgh · Cambridge · Durham

First published in 1992 by
The Pentland Press
5 Hutton Close
South Church
Durham

ISBN 1 872795 53 6

Jacket design by Geoff Hobbs

Typeset by Spire Origination, Norwich
Printed and bound by Antony Rowe Ltd., Chippenham

Acknowledgements

I should like to thank —

The Gurkha Museum for their permission to publish this book about the life of an officer of my regiment, the 5th Royal Gurkha Rifles (Frontier Force) and Lt Col Ivor Edwards-Stuart for writing the Foreword to it.

I should also like to thank —

Brigadier P. R. Prescott for various family photographs of Sir James Stewart which appear in this book.
Lt Col T. Chadburn (13th Frontier Force Rifles) for his excellent photographs of the country North of Gilgit.
Mrs Janet Westenberg for maps of East Africa.
The archivists of the Royal Geographical Society and the National Army Museum for providing me with various maps and photographs.
Brigadier M. Whig, PVSM, FRGS for the photograph of Subadar Kishanbir Nagarkoti IOM.

Books of Reference

The Memoirs of Maj Gen Sir James Stewart.
The Regimental History of 5th Royal Gurkha Rifles, (Frontier Force).
An Outline of British Military History by Major D. H. Cole, MBE MA Litt D, and Major E. C. Priestley, OBE MA.
Encyclopedia Brittanica, 11th edition.
Frontier and Overseas Expeditions from India.

Author's Note

Contrary to those denigrators of our Empire who pontificate to our nation from under their drooping haloes, the British ran a very good Empire. When an Imperial Power attains the status of benevolent authority, under whose protection and guidance its colonial people can advance in security to self-government, the greatest disservice to them is to remove the Imperial shield before they are ready to look after themselves. We have but to think of the chaos in the world today to appreciate the truth of this statement.

The British Empire was established by soldiers, sailors and administrators such as Jimmie Stewart and I do hope this book will reach the hands of young people to give them a true understanding of their gallant and diligent forefathers, who established Pax Britannica throughout much of the world, for the benefit of all.

Jimmie Stewart was commissioned into the Gloucestershire Regiment and saw service in Ireland, but having been rather disillusioned with the thought of peacetime service in England he volunteered to serve with the Indian Army. In his first year in India he was recommended for exploration duties combined with the gathering of intelligence. In his service he was involved in campaigns on the north west Frontier of India, Burma, Tibet and China, East Africa and Aden. His special qualities involved him in expeditions into Kashmir and to the 'Roof of the World' – the Pamirs.

Nowadays we are always excited and rightly filled with admiration by our explorers' feats in high mountains and the polar regions. They enter into these tests of endurance of their own free will, with the backing of sound training and all modern equipment for their endeavours. Let us spare a moment to think of the remarkable achievements of the soldiers of the Royal Fusiliers and the Indian regiments accompanying them in their advance on Lhasa (Tibet), when they fought a battle at Karo La, at an elevation of 16,600ft!

After many requests from his daughter Ursula, Jimmie (General Sir James Stewart) eventually agreed to write his memoirs for her. Some years ago she bequeathed his memoirs to the Gurkha Museum at Winchester and I am indebted to the Museum for their permission to edit and publish this story of an officer of my regiment. I have included further details of military history to show why he became involved in so many exciting and interesting events which took place on our Imperial frontiers.

Robert Maxwell

BOOKS BY THE SAME AUTHOR

Published by The Pentland Press.
3 Regal Lane, Soham, Ely,
Cambridge, CB7 5BA

These books, together with this publication, cover one of the most exciting periods of Imperial History – the story of British India from after the Napoleonic wars to the end of the Second World War. It is natural therefore that reference is made in the current book to related events described in previous books.

DESPERATE ENCOUNTERS — ISBN 0 946270 35 X

THE HINDUSTANI FANATICS
Ambela 1863, Major Battye's Death 1888, Black Mountain 1890
AFGHANISTAN
The Second Afghan War 1878
THE HUNZA – NAGAR CAMPAIGN 1891
THE GREAT WAR
Suez, Gallipoli, Mesopotamia (Later to be Iraq).
NORTHWEST FRONTIER
Waziristan 1920, No 11 Damdil Piquet 1937
THE SECOND WORLD WAR
Iraq and Persia, Italy, Burma

VILLIERS-STUART ON THE FRONTIER — ISBN 0 946270 57 0

The Militia in England 1893, The 93rd Sutherland Highlanders,
The 20th Punjab Infantry, 5th Royal Gurkha Rifles (Frontier Force)
The Tirah Campaign 1897, The Chilas Convoy (Relief of Gilgit)
Innovations and Inventions, The last years before the Great War

VILLIERS-STUART GOES TO WAR — ISBN 0 946270 85 6

The Raising and Command of 9th Battalion the Rifle Brigade
The story of 9/Rifle Brigade in the Ypres Salient 1915
Return to India–
Re-training 1/5th Royal Gurkha Rifles for Mesopotamia
Commanding the Mountain Warfare School,
Raising 3rd bn the Queen's Own Corps of Guides
Inspector-General of India
Frontier Brigadier

Contents

LIST OF ILLUSTRATIONS

MAPS

Foreword

By Lt Col I.A.J. Edwards-Stuart.
President, The Punjab Frontier Force Association

Bob Maxwell is to be congratulated on his editing of these memoirs of Major-General Sir James Stewart. Memoirs, if well written as these are, give a true description of the life and times of the individual concerned.

Sir James' memoirs provide a picture rather different to that shown in such television spectaculars as *The Far Pavilions* and *The Jewel in the Crown*, from which many people form their opinion of the life of the average British officer in India. Even fewer people have any idea of the part Indian troops played in so many of the campaigns in which the British Army was involved. They are not necessarily aware that Indian troops played an important part in the campaigns of the last war in Eritrea and Abyssinia, in the western Desert and in Italy, and that the Indian Army was in the majority in the forces that defeated the Japanese in Burma.

Sir James' memoirs give a fresh and true view of an Indian Army officer's life: service on the Frontier including operations in the Black Mountains and Miranzai; the "Great Game" in the Pamirs; the Chin Lushai expedition on the north-east Frontier; wars in Burma and China; and lastly, in the First World War the operations in East Africa and Aden. Indian troops took part in all of them. Life also included shooting in Kashmir and cheerful winters in places like Lahore, Rawalpindi and Delhi. Add to this a happy marriage and it is possible to see what a full and contented life the average Indian Army officer led. There were, of course, hardships: campaigning in Waziristan in the heat of the summer and the bitter cold of winter; the high instance of disease; and the inevitable separations from wife and family.

These memoirs show that Stewart was not a Roberts, a Kitchener or an Auchinlech, but a run of the mill soldier who put his profession first and was ready to grasp with both hands every opportunity to excel in it. He was a modest man, like so many good soldiers, with no pretensions to superiority over his fellow officers. A good satisfying read.

Ivor Edwards-Stuart

INTRODUCTION

Jimmie Stewart – Frontiersman

At the end of the Napoleonic wars Russia had the most powerful army in Europe – and the Czar was intent on using it to expand his territories to the south and east, including the acquisition of land which would allow him access to the Mediterranean.

Russia was now a threat to India and in 1839 we fought the First Afghan War to prevent the Russians from moving into Afghanistan where they would be on the Indian Frontier.

In 1853 the Czar defeated a Turkish fleet in the Black Sea as the first move in the taking of Constantinople which would have given him access to the Mediterranean. The British and French fought the Russians in the Crimean War (1854–1856) which foiled the Czar's designs.

At this time England's population was less than 15 million, whilst in Ireland the population was about 8 million. It is not surprising therefore that in the British fighting services one man in every three was Irish. Nevertheless our manpower was severely strained to populate, defend and administer our vast empire whilst maintaining the growth of our Industrial Revolution. It was now the turn of the army in India to play a world role and some of the many small wars Indian troops were involved in after the mutiny and up to 1914 are listed below:

Second Chinese War 1859
Ambeyla Expedition 1863
Abyssinian Expedition 1867
2nd Afghan war 1878
Egyptian Expedition 1882
Third Burmese War 1885
Hunza–Nagar Expedition 1891
Tirah Campaign 1897
The Boxer Rebellion 1900

As the years passed by Russia remained a constant threat whilst the British and French Empires lived in 'reasonable' harmony, but by the end of the 19th century Germany began her quest for colonies. These events and many others clearly show that in the years which span Jimmie Stewart's military career there was plenty of scope for adventurous young officers in the Indian Service.

After the Sikh Wars which ended in 1848 the British decided that rather than have another Sikh war their country, the Punjab, would be annexed. The defence of this new territory against incursions by the Afghans – supported by the Russians – together with its policing, would require more troops. The Punjab Irregular Force, known affectionately in the army as the 'Piffers', was formed – later to become the Punjab Frontier Force (PFF). As Russia continued to advance by intrigue and by force of arms towards India the threat to India increased.

In 1858, after the Mutiny, the Indian army was reorganised resulting in an increase in enlistment of Gurkhas and Sikhs. Included in the expansion of the PFF was the raising of a new Gurkha battalion by transferring Gurkhas who had already been enlisted in other PFF regiments. This battalion was to become the 5th Royal Gurkha Rifles (Frontier Force) and Jimmie joined it in 1885.

CHAPTER I

Early Recollections

My father was an offshoot of the Stewarts of Ardvorlich and he is buried at Callander. His main interests were shooting and fishing and sport generally but he inherited sugar plantations in Trinidad which he had to visit occasionally. In Trinidad he married Martha Mogg Allen whose father was the Receiver General there. Her grandfather was the heir to the Viscountcy Allen but at the death of the last Viscount he refused to accept the title on the grounds of the expense of taking it up and supporting it.

In 1861 my parents came home from Trinidad for a short spell in Scotland and I was born near Glasgow on 9th August 1866. We then returned to Trinidad and I have memories of a Negro nurse, Indian coolies, French patois ditties and Indian songs. But my first real recollections are of a sea voyage home after my father's death. I remember there was a tremendous storm in the Atlantic when a man was nearly lost overboard, but was saved by a sailor taking a firm grip of his hair and hauling him back on board.

After a few years in Clifton, Bristol, at my mother's home at High Littleton we moved to Jersey where I started my education at the 'Miss Greaves Establishment'. I then joined my older brother Alick at Clifton College in 1872 before moving, in 1874, to Stoke House, Stoke Poges, where I was to work for a scholarship. Passing this test I moved to Malvern School in 1874 where I was in Rev H. Foster's house until 1878. My teachers thought I had a good chance of getting into the ICS (Indian Civil Service) but I decided that I wanted to go into the army. I passed the army entrance exam without any special preparation and entered Sandhurst in September 1880. Whilst there I played association football for the College and captained the cricket team. I fear that games and sports rather interfered with my work, but I became an Under Officer and passed out all right.

The first idea was that I should go to the Seaforth Highlanders but for various reasons that was given up. I was then asked and agreed to join the Royal Scots Fusiliers; but when the Gazette was published I found myself posted to the old 18th (the Gloucestershire Regiment) – a really fine if rather old-fashioned British county regiment. Later I was offered a transfer to the Royal Scots Fusiliers but being very contented where I was I declined the kind invitation.

Ireland

I soldiered with the Gloucesters in Ireland – a very happy time. I played cricket for the 'Military in Ireland' and I had the use of three horses. We experienced rather troublous times; evictions, patrolling etc, but the military, both officers and men, were popular and were made welcome everywhere.

I travelled in jaunting cars over most of King's County, Galway and Tipperary for dances, tennis and sport. I remember starting for a dance to be held at Nenagh in Co. Tipperary; the major commanding my company and I left our Mess immediately after dinner in pouring rain on a jaunting car and arrived at Nenagh at about 10pm, drenched through. We had to stand in front of a roaring fire for a considerable time before we were dry enough to enter the ballroom. We left Nenagh next morning at about 4am. I fell asleep and at about 7am I awoke to find that the jaunting car had come to a halt; the horse was fast asleep and so were the major and the jarvie. That was no singular experience in Ireland.

Dances were scenes of great hilarity. At a Hunt Ball at Banagher in Co. Galway, in the middle of supper one gay fellow took a blanc-mange and crammed it on a bald pate. When leaving that Ball, most of the men crashed from the front door to the bottom of a long flight of stone steps. At a house in King's County where I was staying after a dance I came down to breakfast soon after 9am, when the butler expressed the greatest surprise and said none of the 'gentry' would be down until midday. He was still more surprised when I said I preferred tea to whiskey.

Games were played in the same light-hearted spirit. In those days girls playing tennis wore bustles. Once in the middle of a hard game a girl dropped her bustle, she was not in the least perturbed, picked it up and hung it on a post with the remark "bad cess to yer".

Real soldiering was not considered. Companies were very weak in numbers, being frittered away on detachments; but shortly before we left Ireland in the winter of 1882 we were made up to full strength by the calling up of reserves in preparation for the Egyptian Campaign and we got some really fine old soldiers.

On our last night at Birr we gave a farewell dance and from the dance I marched straight to the station in the very early hours. We went to Queenstown to embark on the troopship *Assistance*. She was a very old ship and had been condemned for years. As we lay along side waiting to embark while the Buffs were disembarking on the farther side we clamoured for food and drink, but the naval officers told us that we could have nothing until we were actually on board. When on board they treated us nobly.

We had a very bad passage over to Portsmouth, rolling – as the naval officers told us – to within a degree or two of overturning. On arrival at Portsmouth we marched to Clarence Barracks, which also had been condemned for years. So you can see that the authorities did not consider the troops too kindly.

Soon after arriving at Portsmouth I was nearly arrested on the cricket ground in mistake for another officer of my name. Living in Portsmouth was very different from serving in Ireland. No sport, nothing but a run of tea parties and social enjoyments.

I decided to volunteer for the Indian Army and was given embarkation leave.

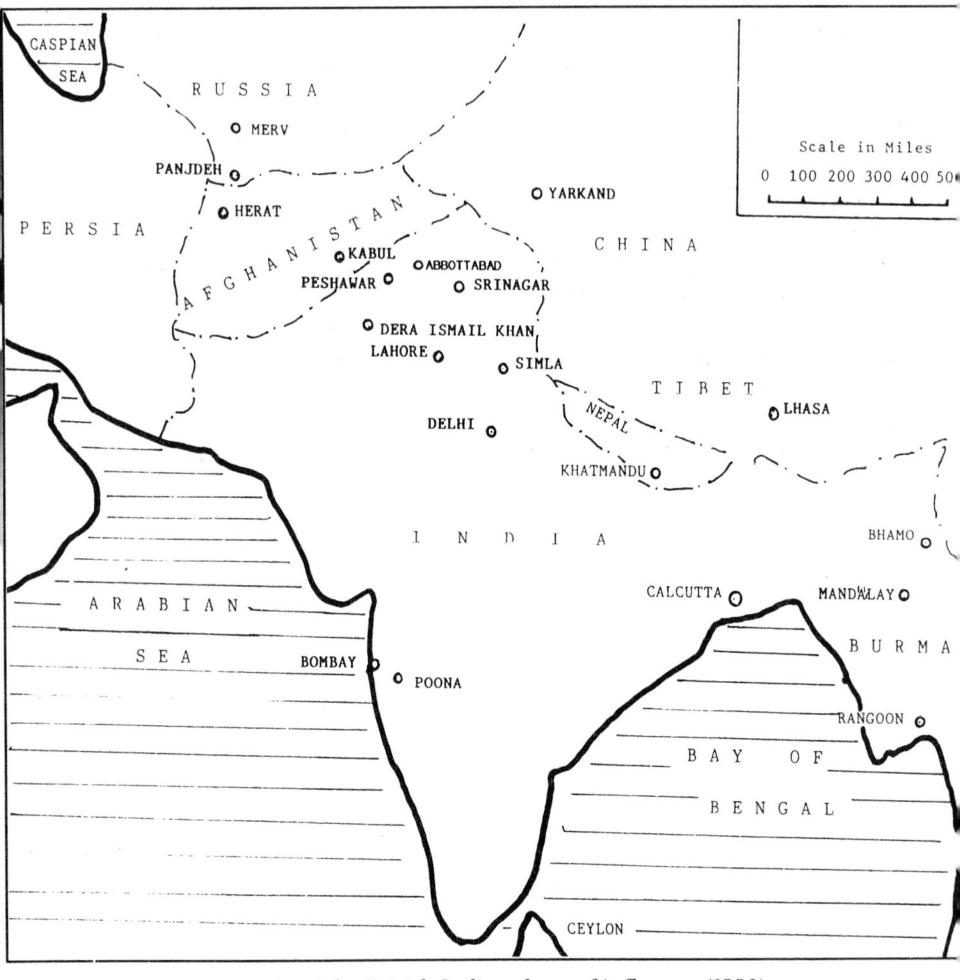

Map 1 — The British India sphere of influence (1880).

CHAPTER II

Arrival in India

I embarked on the transport *Serapis* at Portsmouth in March, 1883.

The voyage was a novel experience. The transport was packed with troops and their wives under conditions which would not be tolerated nowadays, but which most of us thoroughly enjoyed. I, like the majority of the junior officers, shared a cabin in 'Pandemonium', in the depths of the vessel. We depended for air on canvas ventilation shafts because our portholes could never be opened, except in the Red Sea, as we were on or below the water line. Still, we were luckier than some, as the more junior officers had only hammocks to sleep in. For bathing we had sail baths and there was always a fight to get them. The decks were so crowded that deck games were impossible, so we got our exercise by organised promenades. The men were even more crowded, but kept fit and happy.

The wives' sleeping accommodation would seem incredible nowadays. The officer on duty had to go round them, which was indeed an ordeal, especially in the Red Sea and Indian Ocean. *Horresco referens*! The men and their wives were a much rougher lot in those days and enjoyed what would not be tolerated now.

Food was ample but monotonous – no cold storage and so no variety. We all had wonderful appetites and teeth so in between meals we munched ship's biscuits.

In the evenings we often had concerts and other entertainments, and after 'Last Post' we occasionally had grand pillow fights when we from 'Pandemonium' stormed the quarters of the more senior officers on the main decks, and were usually flung back into our depths.

There was all the interest of new places; Gibraltar, Malta, Port Said, the Suez Canal, Aden and at last Bombay. I suppose that of all those places Port Said has changed the most. Then, in 1883, it was literally a sink of iniquity as the worst characters from east and west collected there. We were forbidden to wander about except in parties and even so certain parts of the town were out of bounds. We were glad to get on board again. The canal was narrow and shallow but we squeezed our way through it. Of course all this was of great interest to us; it was our first voyage and there were the camels, the desert, the encampments, and even the flies.

We had several officers on board who had been in the recent Egyptian Campaign (*see* Annexure "A") and they gave us graphic descriptions of their experiences. One gunner colonel laughingly told me how he had got some of his decorations – two medals, a CB and a Medhijee, and he had never heard a shot fired. Still, it fired our imaginations.

On getting into the Indian Ocean we were ordered to wear tropical uniform. I turned out in what I thought was beautiful khaki, only to learn from the other officers that I had been 'planted' by my tailor with what he thought 'suitable'. However, it was well cut and served as an excellent pattern for the Indian tailor to copy.

I took out a very nice bull terrier and he was very fit though he did feel the heat in the Red Sea. He was destined to give me lots of fun and sport but he eventually died of hydrophobia, no doubt picked up from the bite of a mad jackal he had been hunting.

We arrived in Bombay at the end of March and of course were much interested in all the novel sights of India. But perhaps the most striking sight was the face of one of our lot. He appeared in the morning with his face crimson and swollen from mosquito bites. We had begun our education!

We, who had come out to join the Indian Army, went off to the military authorities to get our orders. They had never heard of us, but told us to come back in four days. On the way out we had decided what would be our destination in our own minds. We were all going to the pick of the Indian regiments and I personally had selected a Bengal cavalry regiment, and had worked some interest to secure it. When we returned to the office we found we were all posted to Bombay or Madras regiments – not one of us to Bengal or the Punjab.

I joined the 9th Bombay Infantry in Poona and spent three quite pleasant months with them, learning a bit about the country, the language and Indian soldiering, and going through a riding school to qualify for a Bombay cavalry regiment which I had been invited to join. I acquired an Arab horse from a brother officer, which I did not know had been raced. The first time I took it out on the course I had to ride a severe finish! Later I was told that it always took charge when taken on to a race course.

I also learned the ways of the Indian groom (the syce), now alas completely changed. I used to ride the one or two miles home from parades at quite a brisk pace. The syce always got home with me by dodging through other people's compounds. I suggested to him that he should come more slowly and that I would get someone else to hold my horse until he arrived. He refused this offer indignantly, telling me that he would lose face if he slacked.

Quite unexpectedly, one night in mess a telegram arrived for me, posting me to the 1st Sikhs – a very fine regiment in the Punjab Frontier Force. Everyone in the Mess congratulated me, which made me realise my good fortune. I owed this appointment to Lord Beresford, the Military Secretary to the Viceroy, who had heard from Lady Huntingdon who was a distant relation of mine and had been very kind to me in Ireland.

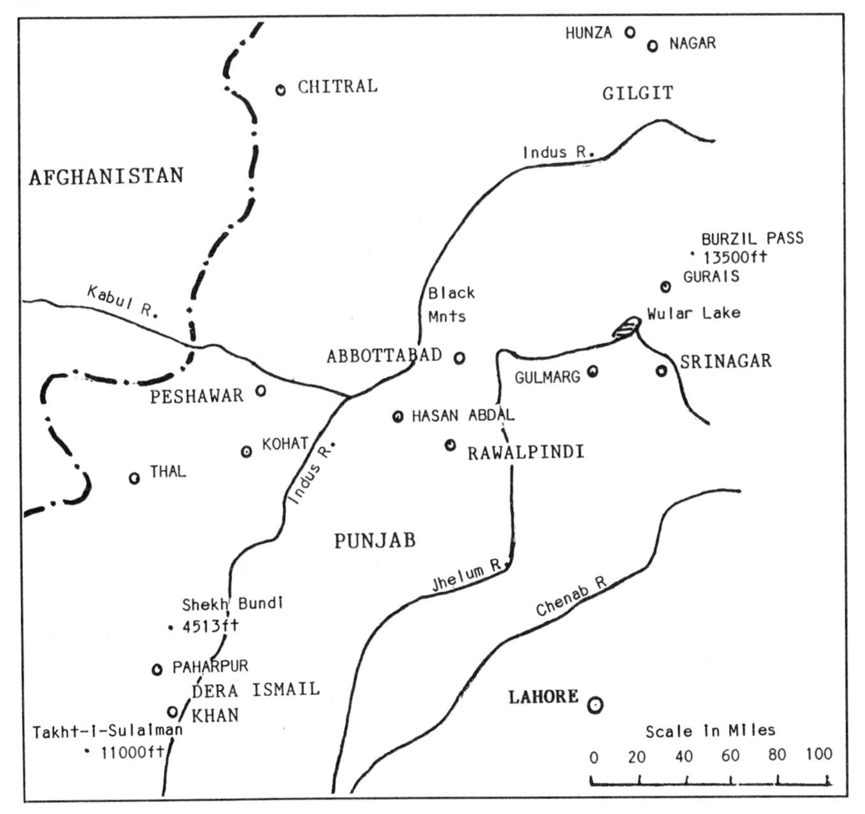

Map 2 — NWF–Punjab–Kashmir.

With the 1st Sikhs

I had an interesting journey from Poona to Abbottabad. Rail to Rawalpindi ('Pindi) and then to Hasan Abdal, where I left the train and was introduced to tonga travel for the 44 mile journey to Abbottabad. En route I had stopped at Delhi where I made a hurried tour of all the historic spots of the old capital of India.

Abbottabad was the Headquarters of the Punjab Frontier Force and was garrisoned by units of that force. My regiment, 1st Sikhs, and the 5th Gurkhas in which I was to spend so many years, and a mountain battery were stationed there and we all shared the garrison mess; a very cheery and sociable arrangement.

The Takht-i-Suleiman Survey Expedition

I had three months in Abbottabad during which I learned a good deal about mountain and frontier warfare. At the end of that time 1st Sikhs were ordered to move to the Frontier. We marched to Dera Ismail Khan (DIK) along the Frontier, cis Indus – a very unaccustomed route and it took us about a month. It was a new experience for me and a most valuable one. We marched always well before dawn so as to arrive in camp before the day got really hot. I learned a lot about transport, the loading of camels and mules, carts and even elephants; the striking and pitching of tents of all shapes and sizes; the feeding on the march of officers and men, all of which was to prove invaluable in the future.

We used to have a great ceremony before sunrise – the time when one could recognise a white horse at thirty yards. The whole Regiment was paraded, the buglers sounded reveille and the guard presented arms. It was very impressive and I think it confirmed the Indian soldiers' belief that we were sun worshippers! I think the custom is now obsolete everywhere.

Along the route that we followed, the villagers had never seen a regiment and few had seen a white man. We were 'honoured' everywhere; offerings for the officers, feasts for the men, and the gathering of some very suitable recruits. In return the Regiment gave band performances, athletics, wrestling contests etc. It was a very cheery time, varied for us officers by a certain amount of shooting but it was a very sandy, desolate country, and so only a few birds.

I mentioned 'recruits', but in those days there were long lists of men waiting to get into the Regiment and no one had a chance unless he was of the right caste, had family connections and exceptional physique, sometimes of wrestling or athletic renown. No Sikh recruits were taken under 5ft 8in and the average height of a Sikh company was about 6ft.

The Regiment always enlisted Pathans, Punjab-Mohammedans, Dogras and a few Oudh Hindus; so I learned a good deal about some of the varied races of India. In my 'forty years in India' I never completed that knowledge – a politician claims to be able to do so in a few weeks in or out of India!

The crossing of the River Indus by a bridge of boats was a novel experience. The Indus near DIK is easily bridged in the cold weather, but in the hot weather when the snows in the Himalayas are melting it becomes a sea and has to be sailed over.

We got to DIK about the middle of November and were at once put under orders for the Takht-i-Suleiman Survey Expedition, so I was soon to get my initiation into frontier warfare. After two or three marches over dead flat country we entered the frontier hills; towering heights on each side of our route which had to be piqueted. There was a little sniping which was certainly disturbing and there was difficulty in finding water. Some of the water had strong medicinal properties which affected men and beasts. Roads had to be made. In one narrow place rocks had to be blasted out before we could get a laden camel through.

Then came the attack on the Takht itself, some 11,000ft high. It took us two days. The crest was lightly held but our mountain 'pop-guns' and Snider rifles soon cleared it. The turning party got lost and for the first and only time I heard buglers sounding "I have lost my way". This was the first time, too, that I had seen a man hit by a Snider bullet. It was indeed an explosive one and the only one which would normally stop a charging frontier tribesman. It is astonishing what wounds they can withstand and recover from. Soon after this the Indian Army was re-armed with Martini-Henry rifles.

We bivouacked on the summit. It was bitterly cold and we had no blankets, but we managed to keep warm, one side at a time, by lying near the blazing trunks of trees that we had cut down.

We were soon back in cantonments at DIK.

Christmas at Lahore

At Christmas I went off with Dallas of 1st Sikhs to Lahore. This was no ordinary journey as we had to travel 160 miles to the nearest railway station at Chichawatni. We did it in a tonga, the ponies galloping all they knew from one stage to another which were about five to seven miles apart. It took us nearly ten hours and it was certainly a very tiring trip. The rail journey on to Lahore was not much better, sandy desert and flies abounding.

Lahore was a very good spot in Christmas week with dinners and dances every night and cricket matches all and every day. There was no polo and very little tennis – cricket was everything. The Punjab Civil Servants entertained everyone, especially officers of the PFF, for in those days the PFF was under the Lieutenant Governor of the Punjab and not the Commander-in-Chief of India. This was supposed to facilitate immediate action in the case of risings etc.

Founded on the same idea was the privilege of officers to dine in their Messes in plain clothes. Such kit as they turned out in! The 'Nuts' in blue serge or some dark suits; the 'Old Brigade' in frock coats and strange waistcoats, and several in 'catch 'em aliveo' garments. There was almost a revolution among the die-hards when Sir Charles MacGregor ordered Mess Dress to be worn. The change was welcomed by us junior officers, and I don't think anyone ever claimed that it hindered our mobilisation!

We got back to DIK for the New Year and for the parade of the whole garrison on New Year's morning, in accordance with the universal practice in India.

Life in DIK

Our garrison consisted of one cavalry regiment, two mountain batteries and four infantry regiments – all PFF units or, as they were generally called, 'Piffers'. It was a most serviceable brigade.

The weather on the frontier was perfect for five months of the year but the rest of the year was 'Hades'. During the cold weather we had a very jolly time; cricket, racquets, tennis, gymkhanas, small race meetings in which I rode my first races, and some shooting.

Early in the year I went off to Rawalpindi on leave to study and pass the obligatory language test in Hindustani. Pindi was full of young officers, all there to pass various language examinations. As it was the largest garrison in India – over 10,000 strong – we had lots of amusements as well as hard work. How well I was to know Pindi in the future! I do not know how many camps, manoeuvres and so on I attended there, in every rank and under every condition; in bivouacs, in small tents, luxury tents, hotels, private houses, and in every sort of weather; in heavy rains, severe cold and intense heat – but I enjoyed them all.

I was back in DIK in May for the start of the hot weather and I soon learned what heat really meant. We were up at daybreak, on parade at sunrise, and then to the swimming baths, where practically all the officers of the garrison collected, and we had great fun. Then to the Mess where we sat under punkhas and ate mangoes and other fruits which had to be brought daily by tongas from the distant railway station. The fruit and drinks were cooled in baskets full of damp straw which were kept swinging by coolies who often squatted on the ground and pulled the ropes with their toes. We had a small amount of ice which had been collected in buckets in midwinter and then stored in pits of over a hundred feet deep – a great luxury.

After we had breakfasted we went to our various regimental offices to do the clerical work. By then it had really stoked up; the air was fiery and the ground red hot. We finished this work by lunchtime, and then retired to our bungalows for such rest as individuals chose. The bungalows were all tightly closed and darkened and punkhas kept going. After tea we emerged for parades or games.

The racquets court was a favourite rendezvous (RV). In those days it was a comparatively cheap game; we played with English balls which had been re-made but were good enough for us. After playing we used to sit under punkhas and drink tonic water just flavoured with gin – an innocuous drink. Then we went up to the swimming baths again, where our servants had brought our mess kit into which we changed, and went in to dinner.

Everyone stayed up pretty late, for we knew that our beds would be fiery hot. Most of us slept under punkhas on the flat roofs of our houses, and the bhistis (water carriers) used to sprinkle water over the beds to cool them down, but they dried almost instantly.

Such were our lives. But everyone seemed to keep fit. Our ills were prickly heat and frontier sores which were a sort of boil and did not heal for months. At that time there was no irrigation in DIK and therefore few mosquitos and little malaria. It was a great relief, though, when September came and with it a marked change in the temperature.

The start of the cold weather was heralded by the arrival of the 'kulan', which are large cranes. These came in with great regularity with the full moon of September. Duck arrived in October and it was a marvellous experience to be the first gun of the season on the big jheel (lake) at Paharpur. At the first shot literally crowds of duck of every kind got up. But they soon got wild and we then depended on flight shooting in the evenings which was excellent sport.

I had my first experience of Markhor (a large wild goat of northern India) shooting on the hills of Shekh Budin. It meant crossing very difficult ground – at least I found it so and crept over some of it in my stockinged feet, but my shikari chose the most precipitous spots to stop and pour water down his throat – without swallowing. A curious accomplishment. He used to dig his toes into crevices to maintain his balance.

Shekh Budin is a solitary hill rising some 4,000ft above the plain. It was an absolutely barren spot but very much cooler than DIK; so several bungalows and a club house of a sort had been built, all of which were fully occupied in the hot weather. There was no water on the hill and it had to be brought up by mules or donkeys from the plains below. Snakes appeared to thrive; there were many of them but I never heard of anyone being bitten. Shekh Budin was not a delectable spot, but the nights were cool.

CHAPTER III

Joining The 5th Gurkhas

One day in 1894 when I was on language leave in Rawalpindi I saw the very picture of a soldier walking along the Mall. A 5th Gurkha perfectly turned out, well-fitted green uniform, forage cap worn at an impossible angle, belts polished like glass, and the man himself excellently set up and moving very smartly. A very cheery Mongolian countenance completed the picture and I had no doubt that here was the regiment for me. I had been very happy in the 1st Sikhs, a really fine regiment, but I recognised that with the one Gurkha battalion in the PFF the chances of active service were greater. The climate of Abbottabad, which was the permanent station of the 5th Gurkhas, was another consideration.

In March 1885 I was transferred to the 5th Gurkhas in Abbottabad. Colonel Fitzhugh and the Adjutant, Chevenix-Trench, had asked me to join them, and Lord William Beresford had again proved to be a friend.

I travelled to Abbottabad by tonga and rail but all my ponies, dogs and heavy luggage had to go by road. The baggage was carried on camels. A young markhor I had acquired travelled in a crate on a camel.

The Parade for Abdur Rahman, The Amir of Afghanistan

The day after I joined the 5th Gurkhas we marched to Rawalpindi for a big camp of exercise and 'Durbar' for which the Viceroy had come to meet the Amir of Afghanistan. It was a great show and my first experience of a large camp. The Regiment presented a splendid spectacle and as it was comparatively soon after the end of the Afghan campaign many of the soldiers had three medals, the Indian frontier, the Afghan Medal and the Kabul-Kandahar Star. A Sikh brigade, consisting of the old 14th, 15th and 45th Sikhs, was a splendid sight. All were in scarlet full dress, every man with a big beard tied up under a huge paggri and standing about

6ft tall, ablaze with medals. Our own brigade was wonderfully smart and impressive. The 1st Gurkhas in red, the 4th and 5th in green; all wearing Kilmarnock caps worn at seemingly impossible angles and everyone conspicuously bemedalled.

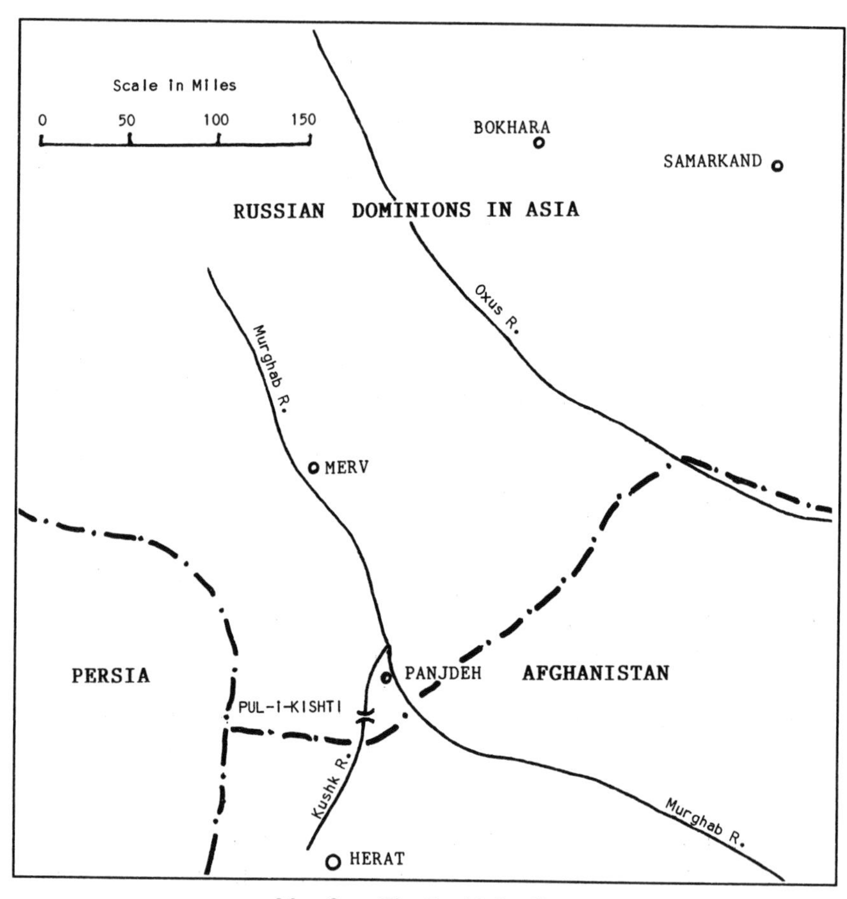

Map 3 — The Panjdeh affair.

The Panjdeh Affair

Soon after the Amir had arrived news reached India of the Panjdeh Affair.

Early in 1884 Russia had occupied Merv, a position which brought her so close to the indefinite boundary of northern Afghanistan between the rivers Oxus and Hari Rud that Russia herself decided it was time to propose a final delimitation of the doubtful line. Great Britain, acting for the Afghan government appointed a commission under the leadership of Sir Peter Lumsden, which in co-operation with a Russian commission would demarcate a frontier acceptable to both parties. On one pretext or another, Russia postponed the start of the work, and used the time to encroach southwards. To watch the Russian moves Afghanistan sent a small force to the Panjdeh area, on the east side of the Kushk river near its junction with the Murghab river at Pul-i-Kishti (Bridge of Boats). In face of the Russian aggression the attitude of the Home Government lacked firmness, with the result that the northern power was emboldened to creep yet nearer to the disputed zone, disregarding its own proposals for a mutual understanding.

The Afghans had moved over to the west bank of the Kushk and the Russian general, Komarov, ordered them to go back to the east bank, which the Afghans were reluctant to do. On 01APR 1885 the Russians attacked the Afghans at Panjdeh inflicting 600 casualties and drove them towards Herat. The news of this outrage was received with indignant protest both in England and in India. It seemed that an insult so gross and wanton could only be met by a declaration of war, and preparations went forward feverishly. War seemed certain and general mobilisation was anticipated.

I was entrusted with galloping into Pindi to find out if we were ‘for it’. I found lists posted up in the Club which showed that we would be in a brigade with old friends of Kabul-Kandahar days; the Seaforth Highlanders and the 3rd Sikhs. We could not have selected finer regiments to serve with.

The camp broke up immediately and we started back for Abbottabad to complete mobilisation. However, there was a change of Government at home, Lord Salisbury’s handling of the crisis averted hostilities and the Russians gave way. The Amir was pacified and the peace secured.

Delhi Manoeuvres

In the autumn the battalion was ordered to Delhi for a big concentration, manoeuvres and a great ceremonial parade. Military representatives attended from all European nations. We were away for six months, on the march and on manoeuvres etc. The Regiment got extraordinarily fit and the marching improved out of all knowledge, mainly through the exertions of the Adjutant.

In the 1930s the standard rate of march of the regiment was 4 miles in the hour. We were very shaken when in Delhi in 1941 we had a brigade exercise of three days duration, in the company of 1/12th Frontier Force Regt and 5/13th Frontier Force Rifles.

They had the habit of marching at 5 miles in the hour! The Gurkha will defeat anyone in speed up and down mountains but on flat ground the 'length of leg' is bound to tell!

Two incidents impress themselves on my memory. At one camp the Gurkhas said they had marked some pig in a bit of jungle. Two or three of us novices thought we would go out and be initiated in pig sticking. The Gurkhas went through the wood but nothing came out of it. We urged them to try again, and there was a shout that they had 'found' but that the pig would not 'break'. The boldest of our number decided to stir the pig with his spear. In he went and there was a dull thud followed by a roar of laughter from the Gurkhas. They had carefully concealed a large log with grass and branches to represent the pig.

The other incident was the death of my bull terrier. He was attended by a vet but no one diagnosed hydrophobia. He had paralysis of the jaw and hindquarters, no doubt dumb madness. My old mohammedan servant, to whom dogs are anathema, nursed the dog with the greatest of care and eventually carried him to his grave, with disregard to all prejudices. In the hot weather in DIK the bull terrier used to lie all day in the bathroom. One day, to amuse himself he pulled my sponge to pieces, for which I reproved him, rather forcibly. A few days later he appeared with a brand new sponge in his mouth. No one had lost a sponge, but one might have been missing from the regimental store. Was he making reparation, or just indulging his taste for sponges?

Back in Abbottabad at the beginning of 1886 I settled down to the ordinary regimental routine, but in May I and an old friend, Duncan of 1st Sikhs, went to Kashmir on six months leave.

Leave in Kashmir

The road to Kashmir from India at that time was not made beyond the bridge over the Jhelum, on the frontier of Kashmir. We had to march on foot while our baggage was carried on mules and by coolies. The path was only a track and there were rest houses every twelve miles or so – the Dak bungalows of India. It was a delightful march, through magnificent scenery and a perfect climate. In about six marches we arrived at Baramula, at the entrance to the Wular Lake. There we got into house-boats and were rowed or pulled up to Srinagar in about three days.

Guide books will tell you all about Srinagar, but in those days life there was very primitive, and living was extraordinarily cheap. One could live on eight annas a day, but we lived luxuriously on one rupee a day.

A rupee was equal to one shilling and eightpence and there were 16 annas in a rupee.

Clothes of Kashmir homespun were almost given away; a suit consisting of coat, waistcoat and plus fours, which was then the universal kit in Kashmir, could be got for about three rupees.

After about sixteen days there we went off to the Lolab Valley and did some shooting; black and red bears, and a little fishing for snow trout. We lived in tents and shifted camp frequently. The country was delightful and at that season there was a lot of fruit; white heart cherries, apples and mulberries galore. Every living thing seemed to thrive on mulberries – men, cattle, sheep, chicken and fish.

When the weather got really hot and rather steamy in the Valley of Kashmir we moved up to Gulmarg which was then a very small hill settlement; it could not even by called a station. There were a few English families there and no games of any kind; very different to the present day when it is a fashionable resort with three golf courses, polo, cricket, tennis etc. We explored the higher hills, many of which were under snow, and did a little shooting of chikor and a very occasional snow partridge.

In September we got back to Abbottabad and to work – and there was lots to be done as we were raising a second battalion of the Regiment, which I was eventually to command.

Simla – Viceroy's Escort

Early in 1888 the Regiment was detailed to provide the Viceroy's Escort in Simla from March to September – a detachment of about 200 men. The Regiment had never performed this duty before and it was selected now on the initiation of its colonel, Lord Roberts, who was C-in-C India. I was detailed to command it and was allowed to choose my own Gurkha officers and most of the men. They were an extremely smart lot and well qualified to maintain – as they did – the reputation of the Regiment.

I remember a few incidents that occurred on the march from Kalka (elevation 2,000ft) to Simla (7,000ft). We did several stages alongside a distinguished British regiment, but they were not accustomed to long uphill marches, and march routine generally. They were decidedly slow over the ground and were inclined to straggle. On one stage we had given them a long start, but soon romped past them well closed up and with all our transport well collected. I heard of this afterwards from some high officials who had driven past us on their way to Simla. They gave us a good mark. We used to start alternately in the mornings and we always got off before breakfast. When our bugles sounded first the British battalion roused themselves and when their bugles sounded first our men lay doggo. So I volunteered to move off silently, and without any bugling, which we found quite easy, it added considerably to the slumbers of our friends.

The British Regiment was very nice to me and insisted on my dining with them every night. This led to a curious experience. One of the majors was credited with hypnotic powers. He had got a few men of this battalion under his influence and was asked to give a demonstration. He agreed to summon one of these men, and a short time later the man dashed into the Mess tent saying he had been called. Not, perhaps, a very sound disciplinary example.

In Simla I think the men created a good impression, and by no means least because they saluted practically every white man in the station. I had told them that Simla was full of officials, for the most part entitled to salutes, and I found the unentitled were loud in their praise of the men's smartness!

But the men got into trouble on two occasions. They had to act as orderlies to various high authorities, theoretically for purely military duties. One man was on duty at the C-in-Cs residence when an Indian 'chuprassi' gave him several hundred letters and a book in which deliveries of them were to be acknowledged. These deliveries would have taken the orderly miles and therefore an ADC was surprised when he returned in a very short time with no letters and no acknowledgements. It turned out that he had put all the letters in a post box and only regretted that he had not been able to get the book in too! The letters were an invitation to a dance.

Another man was orderly to a very popular military secretary, who was fond of entertaining beautiful ladies. This orderly was commissioned to take a very urgent invitation to dinner to a special favourite. She failed to turn up and it was found that the invitation had been delayed in the post. I was hauled up, but soon forgiven and even asked to dinner myself!

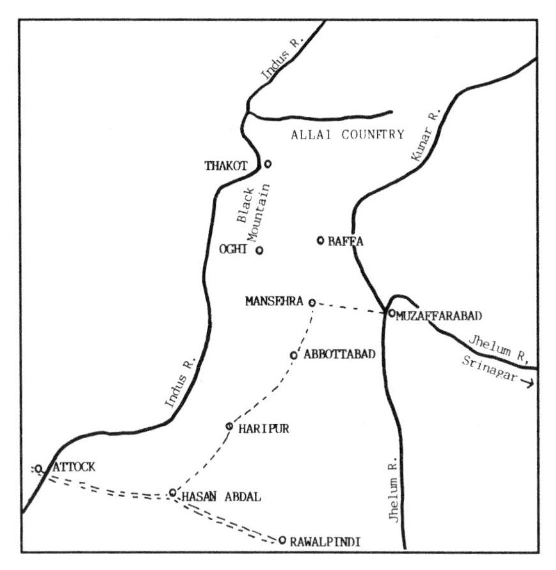

Map 4 — Black Mountain area.

Black Mountain

I had quite a busy time for in addition to my detachment duties I was employed in 'Intelligence Branch'; I had been recommended for this and for exploration work by the colonel of the cavalry regiment in DIK. Still, I was able to play a lot of cricket and football, and had some share in the starting of the Durand Cup, which is still played for annually in Simla; mainly by teams from British regiments.

But all this was interrupted by news that Major Richmond Battye and several men of the Regiment had been killed by frontier tribesmen whilst on a reconnaissance on the Black Mountain (*see* Annexure "B").

The Black Mountain is about 40 miles from Abbottabad and on our special bit of the frontier. So all of us thought that it was our perquisite to take part in the avenging expedition. I represented this to the heads of departments, but they all refused, saying that we had been brought up to Simla for a special duty and must stick it out. I mentioned this to my friend the military secretary who said, 'will you be at the C-in-Cs dance tonight?' When I got there he greeted me with, 'that's all right. You will be off at once'. And so we were, waiting only to be relieved, and then we went off by double marches to Abbottabad and then to the foot of the Black Mountain, where we joined the battalion.

With me I had my Goanese servant who was destined to remain with me until I left the service in 1920. Much merriment was caused in the camp mess by the first letter he received from his home. The post orderly brought in the letter addressed to, "Illustrissimo Signor Don Luis Pedro de Souza, c/o Stewart". After that the distinguished courtesies were reversed!

The attack on the Black Mountain was made in three columns. We were in the Right column with the Seaforth Highlanders and the 3rd Sikhs – a brigade association dating from the Kabul-Kandahar days. We took two days to gain the crest, some 10,000ft, though the defence was slight and consisted mainly of sniping. We had no tents with us and so spent a very uncomfortable first night, as there was torrential rain and our only protection mackintosh sheets.

> Army Headquarters allowed no tents to be carried on operations until December, regardless of where the operations might be. This meant that there were no cook tents for the men whose rations must be cooked, so they had a wretched time. On one occasion fresh meat arrived and with no cooking facilities the men had to eat it raw – saying that it was the best meal they had had for days.

So we were soaked, and in addition the sniping gave us a very disturbed time. But the novelty appealed to us young officers and allayed the discomforts. The second day was rather a trying one for me as I was in charge of the transport which did not reach our camp on the summit until long after dark, and as the route was through thick forest we had a hot time for the last part of the march from snipers and swordsmen.

There was no water on top of the mountain and all had to be brought up from a considerable distance, so our washing arrangements were very curtailed. I never took off my boots, except for short periods during the daytime for about a fortnight and gave my face and hands a very scanty rub over. So, what with the smoke from our fires and the grime and dirt of some of the villages which we destroyed, we were all in a pretty disreputable state when we eventually got off the hill to an ample supply of water, and started the second phase of our operations against some of the other tribes. These took us right down to the Indus and afterwards to the mountains of Allai which were about 12,000ft. Our real difficulties were those of the country. Dense pine forests, precipices, and the merest track over which to advance, but the opposition was almost negligible. Our commanders and troops were experts in mountain warfare – otherwise the enemy would have offered us much tougher resistance. Soon they gave in and agreed to the terms proposed, and we were back in Abbottabad before the end of the year.

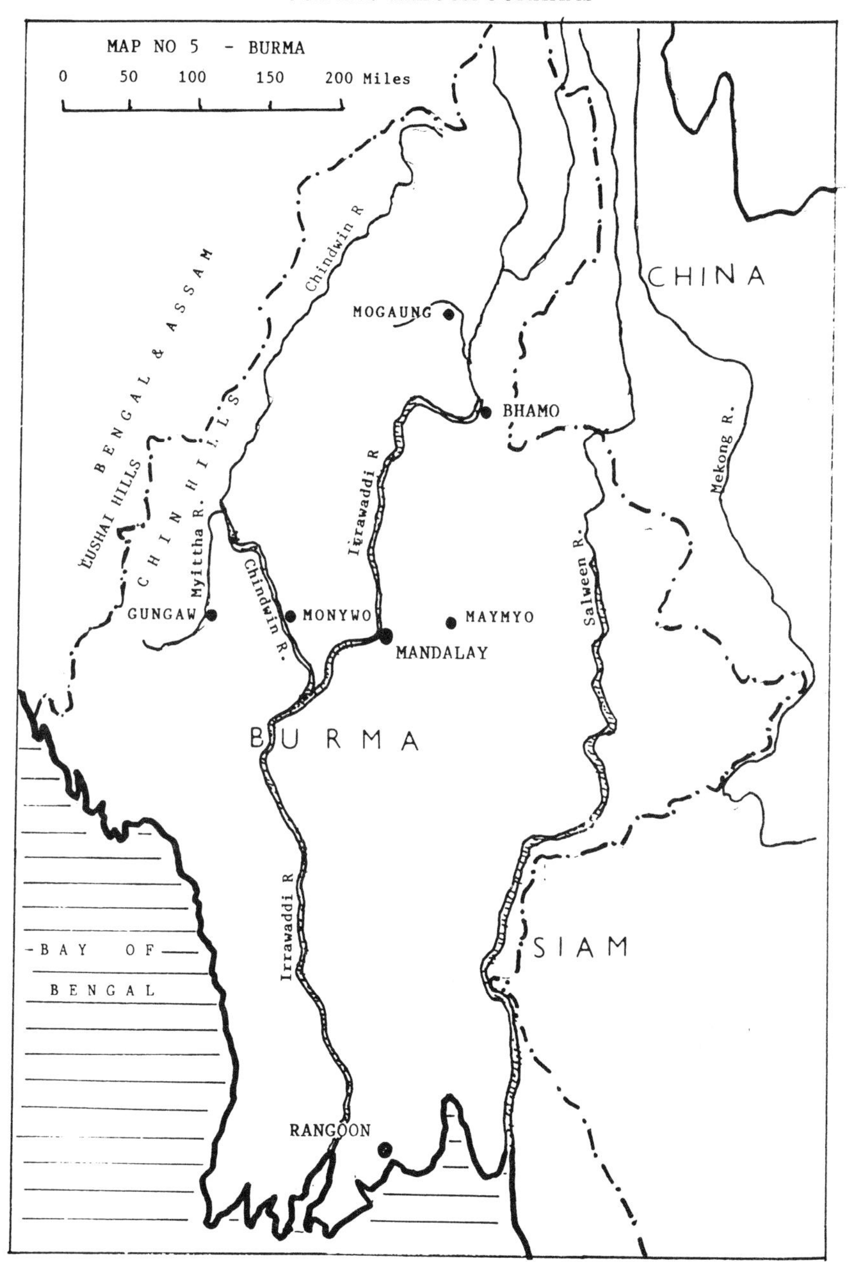
MAP NO 5 - BURMA
0 50 100 150 200 Miles
CHINA
BENGAL & ASSAM
Chindwin R
LUSHAI HILLS
CHIN HILLS
MOGAUNG
BHAMO
Irrawaddi R
Mekong R.
Salween R.
Myittha R.
GUNGAW
Chindwin R.
MONYWO
MAYMYO
MANDALAY
BURMA
BAY OF
BENGAL
Irrawaddi R
SIAM
RANGOON

Map 5 — Burma.

CHAPTER IV

North East Frontier and Burma

The 3rd BURMESE WAR, 1885

France was displaying aggression on the eastern frontier of India, taking advantage of the fact that after the war of 1852 Upper Burma had been left in the hands of the native dynasty. Mindoon Min, the justly respected King of Burma had died recently and had been succeeded by his son Thibaw, a weak and vicious young man entirely under the domination of his consort, Queen Supaya-lat. Probably under her instigation he signalised his accession by a horrible massacre of eighty princes and princesses of the royal family. The British Resident at Mandalay was withdrawn but that did not greatly trouble Thibaw, who was well aware of our present difficulties in Afghanistan and South Africa. He then followed this up by a systematic persecution of British trading interests, while showing special favour to the French, whose Indo-Chinese territory adjoined his own and who were quite willing to slip in by the back door. This was too much for the Indian Government, whose troops under General Prendergast crossed the boundary in November 1885. Thibaw's rule collapsed like a pack of cards, and the north-eastern boundary was firmly consolidated by the annexation of Upper Burma. The country, however, was in such a state of turmoil from Thibaw's misgovernment, and 'dacoity' (gang robbery) so prevalent, that it took a large number of British and Indian units five years before the robber bands were finally dispersed and hunted down. Since then Burma has enjoyed peaceful and prosperous days, only broken by a rising in 1931, until the Second World War destroyed the many years of constructive progress.

I volunteered for service in Burma with the Military Police, and so did Crawford of our 2nd Battalion. We started off in early March 1889 and on arrival I was posted to the lower Chindwin Battalion at Monywo. I had to go up by boat and crossed the frontier into Upper Burma on 1st April. Crawford went up by rail and so crossed the frontier on 31st March. He got the Burma medal, I didn't because the qualifying period ended on 31st March!

I had a very interesting time with this battalion. It was entirely mounted infantry work and meant riding long distances over open, dry tracts of land in pursuit of mostly phantom dacoits. I had only a few months with them before being transferred to the Mogaung Battalion where the work was entirely different. It was mostly in boats and through teak and bamboo forests.

On one occasion I had to take six months' supplies in boats up the Irrawady from Bhamo through the upper defile of the Mogaung. At the upper defile the Irrawady narrows from over a mile in breadth to about 50yds and in the rainy season the river is a surging torrent as the narrow channel becomes an enormous whirlpool. It took me about ten days to get from Bhamo to the far end of the defile. Returning when the river was low in the cold weather is only a few hours' journey. Going up-stream the boats had to cross frequently from one bank to another to avoid the tremendous currents, and in some of the crossings the boats were swept back nearly a whole day's work. When we got to the actual defile all the boats were collected in the shelter of a rock, and were passed through one at a time. The boatmen were fully occupied keeping their boats off the rocks while some 50 to 60 men hauled on ropes attached to the bow of the boat to coax it up river.

On one occasion, when a boat met the full force of the river the bows gave way as the men hauled on the rope. The greater part of the boat was swept downstream, sank, and then re-appeared before sinking finally about one mile below. As the boat sank the steersman jumped into the river; his friends on the rock pushed in poles which the swimmer caught hold of so that he could be pulled to safety. When the next boat was ready for the passage no steersman would take on the task, until finally the steersman of the sunk boat volunteered. He got into the waiting boat and brought it safely through the defile. A very gallant action.

I made one long ride up to the Chinese frontier during which we never saw the sun or even the sky for six days because the forest was so dense. And then I was surprised to hear that I had been appointed Orderly Officer to the GOC, Chin Lushai Expedition. I discovered that this was entirely due to the kindness of Lord Roberts. Burma was then under the C-in-C Madras, who at once raised objections as he thought the appointment should go to one of his Madras officers and that I should have been left to complete my time with the Military Police. Eventually these objections were overruled and I was able to continue my journey on which I had already started. I took up my new appointment with General Penn Symons at Gungaw, at the foot of the Chin Hills.

The Chin Lushai Expedition

At Gungaw during December 1889 our brigade gradually assembled. It was to combine with another brigade advancing from the Bengal side through the Lushai Hills, the two brigades being under the command of Brigadier General Penn Symons.

In preparation for the advance the Myittha river had to be bridged and communications improved. To build the stone piers for the bridges some Naga coolies were employed. Before they left their homes their wives had provided them with strange ornaments which were supposed to ensure fidelity. Such ornaments were worn only by the Naga tribe and were practically unobtainable, though one was acquired by a senior officer at a very large price. I do not know how the vendor accounted for its loss to his lady love.

Ordinarily these Naga coolies wore no clothes, but for decency and on account of the chilly mornings we had provided them with blankets. On entering the water they discarded their blankets. The Burmese ladies used to bathe nearby; they wore only one garment – a sort of petticoat out of which they slipped most discreetly as they sank into the river, putting the garment on their heads. But when the Nagas threw off their blankets, displaying their ornaments, it was too much for the ladies. They forgot all their modesty and stood up in the river shouting with laughter. The joint demonstration lives in my memory!

Our column's primary task was to deal with the Chins, while the Bengal Column advanced against the Lushais. The Chins were utterly uncivilised and possessed hardly any firearms but used spears and bows and arrows, sometimes poisoned, which were very effective in their densely wooded hills. They had given a lot of trouble by raiding into Burmese territory and carrying off men and women as slaves. Among their captives was a very fine specimen of an Irishman with fiery red hair. This appealed greatly to the Chins, so they decided to improve their breed by mating him *nolens volens* with a considerable number of their womenfolk. He was thankful to be rescued! They were an extraordinarily dirty race and of poor physique. Their customs too were degraded; headhunters full of strange superstitions, excessively given to drinking rice beer and consumers of tobacco juice. They made their women smoke pipes with detachable bowls underneath, into which the nicotine drained and was subsequently swallowed by the men.

The opposition we met was slight and our main difficulties were physical – bamboo forests through which we had to cut our way and make tracks sufficient for our mule transport, ponies, bullocks and coolies. We carried no tents, but the Gurkhas, Burmese, Nagas and other coolies made shelters quickly at each halt. The

Chins made one or two attempts to attack us at night, but they were driven off easily.

I remember one night when they attacked a Gurkha piquet. The General and his staff were sleeping in a shelter. As firing broke out he insisted on going out to the piquet which was being attacked, though I tried to persuade him not to. The Chins bolted as we came up. The General's only regret was that he had no shotgun as he could have made sure of getting 'a right and a left'.

We used to protect our posts by cutting an open space all round them. Nothing would induce the Chins to cross this as they felt sure that devils were lurking on the other side. We weren't the devils they feared!

In one of the villages which we had captured, the inhabitants were full of curiosity about all our belongings, equipment etc. They induced one of our men to show them his rifle. By some strange chance the rifle went off, and a man's head was blown to bits. This nearly caused hostilities to break out afresh and the villagers demanded the surrender of the man who owned the rifle. He was to be sacrificed – and I am not sure that he did not deserve to be. A considerable money compensation secured a settlement.

All the troops were employed in road making, which meant the turning up of virgin soil. At the time this was considered to be the reason for the intense malaria of a most virulent type which attacked almost everyone. I do not remember seeing many, if any, mosquitos and there seemed to be few breeding grounds for them. From that experience and several subsequent ones I have often wondered if anopheles are the only cause of malaria. Only a few officers and men escaped malaria at that time, and many of them suffered fatal attacks from it after the expedition.

We had a wing of 2/4th Gurkhas with us and at one time every one of their officers was incapacitated, so Penn Symons, remembering that I belonged to a Gurkha regiment, sent me to command them temporarily. During this period we had to attack a Chin position, which was on a small hill with long grass in front of it. We were in the front line and there had been no firing, when I heard a Gurkha shout that he had been wounded. I thought he must be shamming but when I got to him I found that his thigh had been run through by a 'panji', which is a bamboo stake whose point is sharpened and then hardened in the fire. In the long grass there were a good many of these big stakes, together with small ones capable of piercing an ordinary boot. We advanced with considerable caution and the Gurkhas cleared the way with their kukris. They also rapidly dismantled a bamboo stockade. In a few weeks we occupied their principal villages, Yokwa and Kaka, and then joined hands with the Lushai Column. Peace was delayed for a few days because the chiefs had drowned their sorrows in a flowing bowl. They were hopelessly drunk and we just had to wait until they were sober enough to accept terms.

The expedition came to an end in April 1890. I was recommended for a DSO – which did not come through – and returned to my regiment. But I kept getting attacks of malaria and in June the doctors decided to send me to England.

I had been out over seven years, so I was quite pleased to go and had a jolly time, in between bouts of malaria. However they did not stop me getting an 'Extra' (Distinguished) Certificate on a course at the School of Musketry at Hythe. My last bout of malaria was when I was out with staghounds on top of the Quantocks.

CHAPTER V

North West Frontier 1891

Black Mountain

In January 1891 I heard that there was to be an expedition on the north west Frontier, once more against the Black Mountain tribes. I thought I might get employed even if my regiment did not go, so I obtained permission to return to India before the expiration of my sick leave. I was back in Abbottabad by the middle of February and heard that Mahomed Aslam, the Afghan Commander of the Khyber Rifles, had been severely injured and that I had been given temporary command.

The Khyber Rifles

The Khyber Rifles are a corps of transfrontier Pathans – almost entirely Afridis. Their raison d'être is to safeguard the Khyber Pass while caravans are passing through. They had volunteered for service against the Black Mountain tribes and, mainly for political reasons, their service had been accepted.

Readers may be surprised that an Afghan should have been the Commander of the Khyber Rifles, a British corps. In 1988 I attended the annual reunion lunch of the Punjab Frontier Force Association in London and was sitting at table next to a Colonel of the Guides who was an Afghan. I asked him why an Afghan should be in a British Indian regiment. He replied, 'Oh, every good Afghan wanted to serve in the Guides!'

For me it was a curious experience. The men were of splendid physique and perhaps too full of dash, and liked to encourage themselves by rather indiscriminate firing. But their spirit and keenness were remarkable and they were bent on playing up to their British officer, and looking after his safety and comfort to the best of their ability. Not a man could speak Hindustani. Pushtu was the only language, so it was lucky that I had passed the Higher Standard examination in that tongue. These men were decidedly proud and independent. I had a very fine orderly and at the end of the expedition I gave him, in accordance with the usual custom, a present of some Rs 10. I learned afterwards that he had presented my Goanese servant with whom he was on very good terms a parting gift of Rs 15!

We had many independent posts and even when we joined the main force we were camped well away from them for sanitary and perhaps disciplinary reasons. I was constantly afraid that we might come under fire from our own rather jumpy units! Some of the commanders and units were very new to frontier warfare and had secured for their principal encampment the unenviable title of 'Fort Funk'. In reality there was very little opposition and a rather unusual want of enterprise on the part of the tribesmen.

After a little over a month the expedition came to an end and I took the Khyber Rifles back to Peshawar and handed them over to their permanent commandant.

The Second Miranzai Expedition, 1891

Meanwhile trouble had broken out on another part of the frontier near Kohat. I joined my own battalion, 1/5GR, which had been detailed for this expedition.

Travelling towards the Kurram Valley from Kohat the route lies for some miles on the left bank of the Kohat Toi. 15 miles west of Kohat that stream is joined by the Khanki River, and in the angle between them the Samana Ridge has its beginnings, to continue westwards for some 20 miles at a height of 2,000 to 3,000 ft above the Miranzai plain. North of the Samana three streams run parallel from west to east; the Khanki, the Mastura and the Bara. The watersheds between them comprise long parallel ridges, moulded in much the same pattern as the Samana itself, and bounding the horizon on the north stretches the white panorama of the Safed Koh mountain range.

Of the inhabitants of this part of the frontier, the several divisions of the Orakzais occupy the Samana Ridge, the Khanki Valley, and the greater part of the Mastura valley beyond; while to the north of them the Bara, Bazar and Khyber Valleys, Maidan and the Kajuri Plain are inhabited by Afridi clans. During January and February of 1891 certain Samil sections of the Orakzais had been compelled to

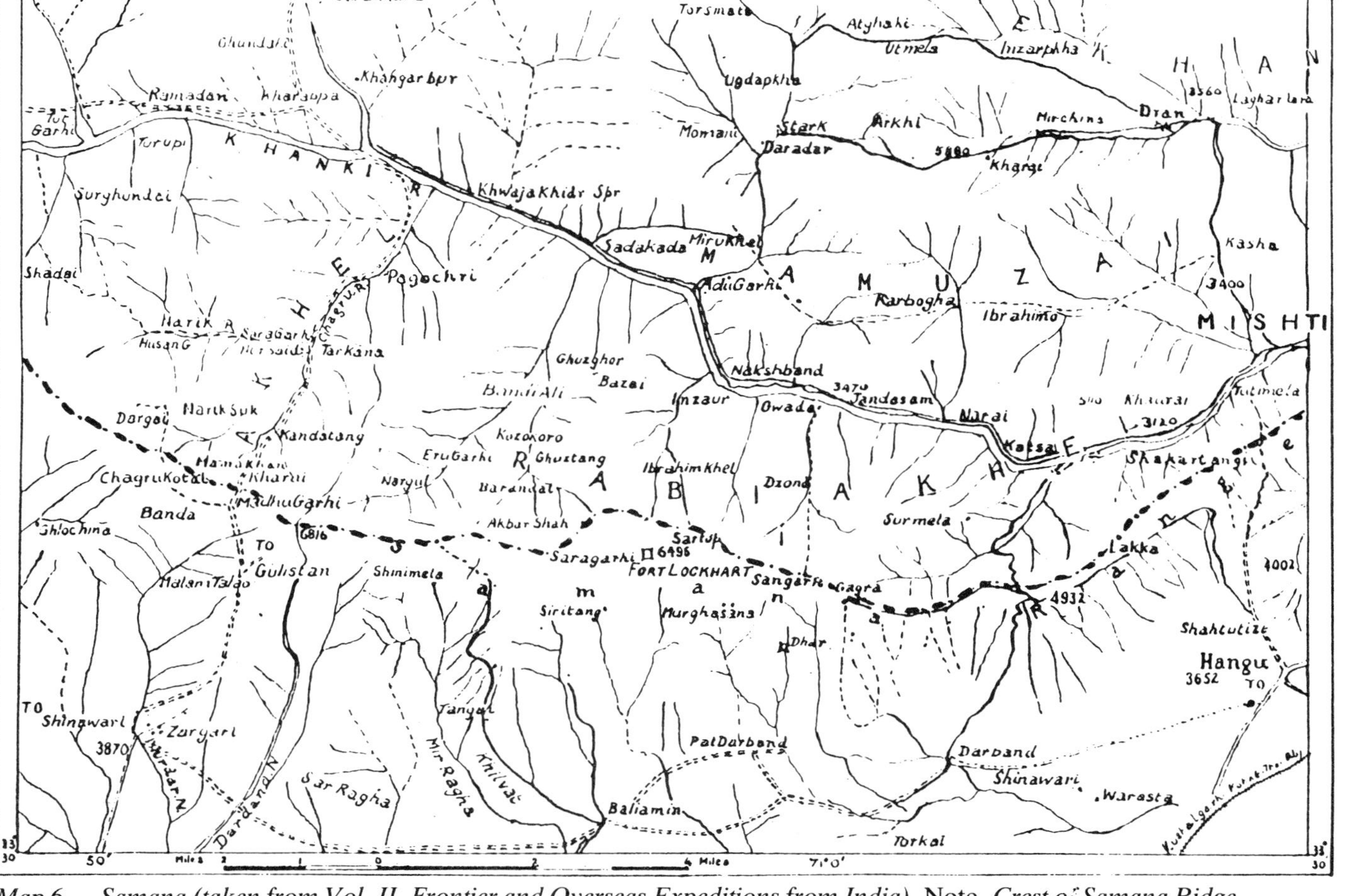

Map 6 — *Samana (taken from Vol. II. Frontier and Overseas Expeditions from India).* Note. *Crest of Samana Ridge indicated by chain – dotted line.*

make restitution for various previous misdemeanours and to tender complete submission by a force under the command of Sir William Lockhart. Under the terms of the agreement entered into at the close of the campaign they consented to the establishment of British posts and the construction of roads on the Samana Ridge. To give effect to this clause of the agreement, when the punitive column withdrew from Orakzai territory, working parties were left on the Samana, and the 29th Bengal Infantry were detailed for their protection.

Not unnaturally the occupation of the Samana by British troops was regarded by the Orokzais as a whole – and even by a number of Afridi sympathisers – as a threat to their independence. They taunted with cowardice those sections that had recently accepted the terms and so worked on their feelings that on 04APR they contrived surprise attacks on the widely dispersed escorts and drove them from the ridge.

No time was lost in initiating retaliatory measures. Sir William Lockhart was then commanding the reserve brigade of the Hazara Field Force at Darband on the Indus. Having been selected to command the troops for this second Miranzai operation he left Darband and on 07APR his brigade began its march to Kohat, accompanied by all its transport.

To return now to 1/5GR in Abbottabad. Whilst orders were received on 06APR to join the column there was a delay of two days whilst transport could be collected. That problem solved, the battalion left Abbottabad on 08APR. Marching by double stages they reached Hasan Abdal on the 9th and then moving by train as far as Kushalgarh, they arrived in Kohat on 11APR.

Hangu, at the foot of an outlying feature from the main Samana ridge, had been selected as the Assembly Area for the expeditionary force and concentration had been completed by 16APR. The force was divided into three columns and of these column 1 was placed under command of our Commandant, Colonel Sym; the command of the battalion devolving accordingly on Captain A.R. Martin. In the operations which followed we are concerned mainly with the activities of Colonel Sym's column, composed of No. 3 Mtn Bty RA, 1/Kings Royal Rifle Corps (KRRC), one half of No. 5 Coy Bengal Sappers and Miners, 1st Punjab Infantry, 27th Bengal Infantry and 1/5GR.

The Capture of Samana, 17th–20th April 1891

The advance began on 17APR, Column 1 moving directly on Lakka which is on the crest of the Samana, whilst the other columns moved along the base of the ridge as far as Darband. Column 1, led by 1/5GR reached Lakka unopposed and from there Sir William Lockhart directed Column 2 onto the Darband Kotal and Column 3 onto Sangar. The route of Column 1 now lay along the crest of the ridge. On reaching the Darband Kotal it was found that Column 2 had arrived, and strengthened by 27BI it was sent down to Gwada, a village due north of Sangar, on the right bank of the Khanki.

Column 1 then continued its advance and on reaching Tsalai found itself opposed by small bodies of the enemy which were strongly posted amongst the rocks. 1/KRRC who were now leading took the position in their stride, but with the loss of their colonel, wounded, and several of their men. From Tsalai it did not take long to reach Sangar where Column 3 was encountered, and there they bivouacked for the night.

Mastan is the name given to that part of the Samana interposing between Sartop and Gulistan. It may be described as a narrow, undulating plateau, opening out in places to a breadth of several hundred yards, rocky for the most part, and covered here and there with coarse grass and scrub, which holds an infrequent black partridge and an occasional hare. It fell to a combined movement of Columns 1 and 3 on 18APR. There was a sharp skirmish when Sartop was reached but as 1/5GR was not involved the details need not concern us.

Column 3 was left holding Mastan and Column 1 withdrew to Sangar. On 19APR Column 2 moved from Gwada to Sangar, Column 1 remained halted but Column 3 found itself opposed by large bodies of tribesmen who had collected for the purpose of recapturing the ridge. Column 3 being widely dispersed along the ridge Colonel Brownlow lacked a striking force to deal with the enemy and so on 20APR he was sent from Sangar the Peshawar Mtn Bty, 2 Punjab Infantry and four companies each from 1/KRRC and 1/5GR. These reinforcements reached Colonel Brownlow at a point east of Saragarhi at 1330hrs and he at once prepared for an attack on Saragarhi to be carried out by 1/5GR with 1KRRC in support, and arranged for a simultaneous assault on the neighbouring village of Ghuztang.

Captain Martin's orders were to attack and clear Saragarhi village, then to capture and clear the hills beyond, and to hold on to the ground captured until the towers of Saragarhi village had been destroyed.

Now Captain Martin was a past master of the art of mountain warfare, with a particular penchant for the arme blanche. Making a rapid study of the ground he directed his leading companies to advance by a covered way and supported by the fire of the Mtn Bty they succeeded in getting close to the enemy without being detected by them. Then while the skirmishing companies dashed forward with bayonets fixed, the remainder opened a devastating fire at short range on the tribes thus taken by surprise. The piquets surrounding the village were taken in the charge, the half-battalion swept through and the enemy fled in all directions, leaving their dead and wounded on the ground and throwing away their rifles as they rang. The momentum of their spirited advance carried the men of 1/5GR beyond the village and straight through to the hills beyond. These they held while Saragarhi and Ghuztang were destroyed with their towers and then, their work completed they returned to Sangar.

The whole affair had lasted but half an hour and the losses in the battalion were only two men seriously wounded whilst the enemy casualties were about 60 killed and 240 wounded. This phenomenal success was due to the element of surprise introduced in the original plan of attack, the élan displayed by the men, and the terror inspired in the enemy by the threat of the bayonet.

The battalion received the warm thanks of Column 3 commander, Colonel Brownlow. Short as the action was and few as were our casualties, 20APR is deservedly kept as a regimental holiday.

For Column 1 the next few days proved uneventful but Columns 2 and 3 were employed in operations beyond Gulistan in the vicinity of the Chagru Kotal, and a number of villages on the northern slopes of the ridge were destroyed. The Afridis sent in a jirgah on 24APR and terms were also made with one or two sections of the Orakzais.

Hearing that the Alisherzai and Mamuzai sections of the Orakzais were inclined to tender their submission, Sir William decided to improve the occasion by first showing the flag in their country of Sheikhan. The settlements in this tract are to be found clustered for the most part in the Lagardara and Daradar valleys, and access to them is gained by the Kharai pass. Before departing on this advance one company of 1/5GR was ordered to march from Sangar to Chikarkot on 27APR to relieve 1/4GR in the posts on the L or C between Hangu and Chikarkot. It was then decided to relieve them as they were required back at Hangu in time to accompany Column 3 on the trip to Sheikhan. This involved the company completing a march of 42 miles in 36 hours in far from favourable conditions. Arriving at 2000hrs at Hangu they were ready to move with the battalion in Column 3 the next morning. The foray to Sheikhan being completed satisfactorily the battalion returned to Hangu on 15MAY, rejoining Column 1 on 16MAY.

The Second Miranzai Expedition was written down as one of the most successful small wars ever fought on the frontier. No further work being required the force was disbanded and the battalion arrived back in Abbottabad on 14JUN.

'Bullets' becomes Subadar-Major

The Subadar Major is the senior Gurkha in a Gurkha battalion (*see* Annexure C).

CHAPTER VI

Gilgit and Beyond

The year of 1891 was to be a very active one for me. In June, shortly after the battalion had arrived back from the Samana, I received orders for special duty in Gilgit – some 200 miles beyond Kashmir.

The military ineptitude of Kashmir had led to the re-establishment of the Gilgit Agency, and at the same time special officers were detailed to supervise the training of the Dogras and Gurkhas, who made up the rank and file of the Kashmir Imperial Service Troops.

I made a hurried journey to Gilgit, crossing the passes from Kashmir – the Tragbal (11,800ft) and the Burzil (13,500) – quite easily at that time of the year. It was to be a very different story on my return journey in October. But it was rough going on the road, or rather track, which was under construction, and mules and ponies got through with some difficulty.

I and three other British officers – one being Townshend, afterwards of Chitral and Kut fame – set to work to improve the Kashmir troops then in Gilgit. They were quite a good lot but lacked training.

Soon we learned that government had sanctioned an expedition against the Hunza – Nagar tribes who had given a lot of trouble in the Gilgit area. Then I heard that as a backbone of the local troops two companies of my own battalion were being sent up. Naturally I wanted to stay and see the expedition through with them, but it was not to be. I had to return to Abbottabad to continue as adjutant, as I had promised my colonel so to do.

A small expedition occupied Hunza and Nagar – two small principalities lying close to the Pamirs and Russian territory, the chiefs of which claimed a dubious descent from Alexander the Great – and had also been adopting a dubious policy. This was one of the passes through which the Russians might have entered Indian

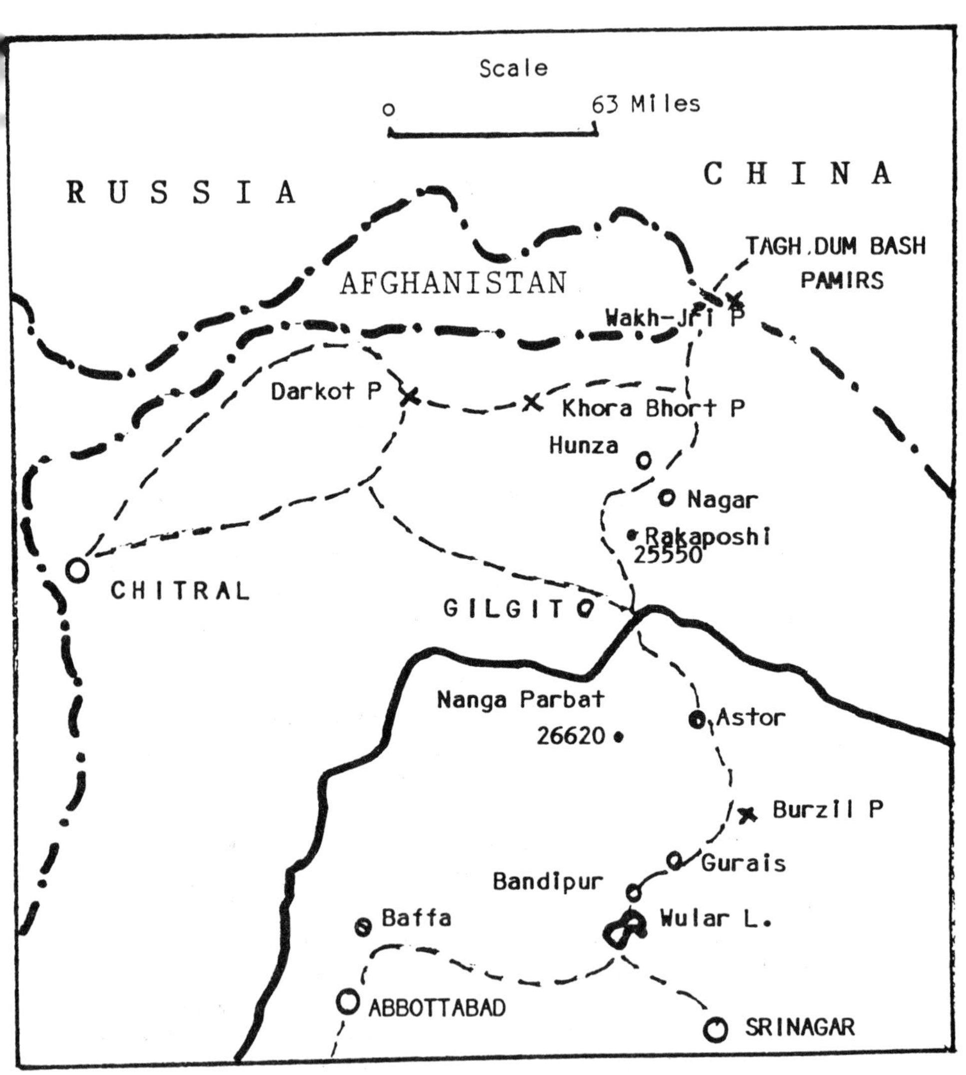

Map 7 — Gilgit and beyond.

territory but the action of the above mentioned expedition had, as a Russian statesman said, '. . . Slammed the door to India in our faces'. This was the Hunza–Nagar Expedition of 1891, which is fully covered in *Desperate Encounters.*

Trouble in the Pamirs

To return to my story.

Meanwhile there was trouble in the Pamirs. F.E. Younghusband (afterwards Sir Francis) of the Central India Horse, who was acting as British Agent in Yarkand, got news of a small Russian force which was exploring towards Chitral. He had no armed men with him, but made a spirited dash to intercept the Russians. In this he succeeded, but after quite a friendly meeting he was suddenly ordered by them to withdraw from undemarcated territory. Having no alternative he retired to the Tagh-dum-bash Pamir, then in the Chinese sphere of influence. He sent urgent messages down to Gilgit, asking for some armed men to be sent up to him. This resulted in me being sent to join him.

I had about 20 men of the 20th Punjabis with me, and my two Gurkha orderlies. I was given distinct orders that if I encountered any of the Russians on the southern side of the Hindu Kush I was to order them to withdraw, and if they refused to do so I was to fire on them. Some Russians had crossed over, but had retired before my arrival, and so I was deprived of the chance of bringing on an Anglo-Russian war!

I had a rather difficult journey to the Tagh-dum-bash as the rivers were in flood. As the normal route usually followed the river beds this meant long detours, sometimes amounting to several days' extra journey. With the melting snow the rivers and streams were ice cold and the currents very swift. Also the river/stream beds were full of boulders which made their crossing precarious. The Chitralis and other natives of the area usually crossed on ponies, riding two on each pony. One of my Gurkhas, in full marching order, thought he would follow their example and for the first time in his life he got up on a pony, behind a Chitrali. In midstream the pony stumbled, the Gurkha clutched the Chitrali and all I then saw were the Gurkha's boots and the butt of his rifle. However he and all his equipment were safely brought to the far bank.

I crossed the Darkot, the Khora Bhort and the Wakh-Jri passes, and so joined Younghusband, to his considerable relief as he thought he might be scuppered any time by the Hunza tribesmen.

The crossing of the Darkot pass, which is 15,000ft high, was difficult as we ran into heavy snow and had to halt for the night near the top of the pass. We scraped the snow off some rocks and then the men and animals spent the night on these cleared spaces. I was lucky to have a small tent d'abri over me. We had to start again before daybreak so as to cross the frozen snow while it was still hard. I was never nearer to frost-bite myself, but the Chitrali drivers managed to tie up our baggage and load their animals, even though all the ropes were stiff with ice.

We had a very bad time too crossing the Chitabui glacier before we got to the Khora Bohrt Pass. This lay in a narrow valley between high steep and barren hills, with a howling wind blowing through. In the valley are two small lakes, the drainage of one going into the River Oxus and so on to the Caspian sea; the drainage of the other going into the Gilgit river and so to the Indus and the Indian Ocean. A strange divergence from almost the same source. On this glacier my Goanese servant nearly lost his life. He was absolutely frozen but recovered quickly when we got him into camp and gave him hot tea. He had a bad time later on when we were crossing the Khora Bohrt on our return journey. Snow was falling heavily and he with some others got rather exhausted. In no time they became drowsy, sat down, and were soon enveloped in snow. They were discovered just in time by some of our Punialis, who had gone back to see what had become of them.

I think I was the first European to cross the Khora Bohrt Pass, and the information I gained was decidedly useful to our intelligence branch. Crossing the passes I depended greatly on yak transport. Some of these animals had never carried loads before, but the Puniali tribesmen who were with me were marvels in managing and loading them.

Younghusband and I waited on the Tagh-dum-bash until we had made certain that the Russians had withdrawn completely and then, as transport was insufficient I went ahead, sending back yaks to bring him along later.

While we were on the Tagh-dum-bash I did a little shooting but as we were on Chinese territory uninvited, it was inadvisable to let off our weapons too frequently. 'Oves poli' abounded and I saw some large herds of them, but they were too wild. I picked up some big heads and also a few good ibex. These were all stacked outside my tent and later brought down to me in Gilgit by local carriers. I never recovered them from there. They were, I believe taken away as trophies by a distinguished author and newspaper correspondent.

I travelled to Gilgit by forced marches, riding 80 miles on the last day – not too easy on these mountain tracks. I had to hurry as I heard that the Viceroy, Lord Lansdowne, was in Srinagar and was anxious to get first hand information about the Russian incursion, so I pushed on by double marches.

Crossing the Burzil Pass was very difficult. I got to the foot of the pass and found that the first snow of the year had started to fall. The villagers assured me that if I did not cross the pass that night I might be held up for a week or more. So I determined to make the attempt that afternoon. As I got to the crest at nightfall I caught up with a convoy of several hundred bullocks, returning to India after bringing supplies up to Gilgit. They were in the greatest trouble as neither the beasts nor their drivers had ever seen snow before and were quite bewildered. The track had been obliterated, but I gradually pushed to the head of the convoy, leading my pony and with my dogs carried by my syce and another servant. I made a lucky cast and found the trace of the new road a little way below, and after seeing the convoy onto it I descended rapidly to the first village. That night the convoy lost 50 drivers and about 50 bullocks.

Getting to the village about 0200hrs I found a very old friend and a most hospitable one. He was Frank Duncan, generally known as 'Fanny' Duncan. He had been at Sandhurst and in the Gloucestershire Regiment with me but was now in 23rd Sikh Pioneers. Fanny invited me to take off my boots and clothes and to jump into his bed to get warm, while his servant prepared hot cocoa and some food pending the arrival of my baggage. I readily accepted and he howled when my ice cold feet touched him. When I told this story years afterwards at a Women's Institute meeting there were long faces until I established the real sex of 'Fanny'!

Duncan had tried to cross the pass that afternoon but had been driven back by the snow and high wind. My servants and baggage arrived a few hours later but required a day's rest after all their hardships.

Crossing the next pass – the Tragbal – I met the detachment of my Regiment on their way up to Gilgit. A week later they had a very hard time getting over the Burzil Pass and had many cases of frost-bite, including their commanding officer, Barrett – later to be Field Marshal Sir Arthur – who lost two of his toes. They were rewarded for their hardships however for they gained much glory in the subsequent Hunza–Nagar Expedition; Boisragon winning the VC and Badcock a DSO after being recommended for a VC, while many of the men won decorations for gallantry. Another brother officer, Manners-Smith, though detached from the Regiment also won a very good VC.

When I got to Bandipur on the Wular Lake my difficulties were over. I found boats waiting for me which took me to Srinagar where I was received by the Viceroy, and I gave him a full account of all that had happened.

I had had to wait some time at Bandipur for my baggage party to arrive. At the head of it marched my Goanese servant, clad in the best European shooting costume. When the Kashmiri boatmen saw him they shouted, 'Here comes the Lord Sahib (the Viceroy)'. They had to pay for their humour for it infuriated Luis, who belaboured them freely.

From Srinagar I hurried on to Abbottabad where the Commander-in-Chief, Sir Frederick Roberts, was inspecting troops and wished to see me. He was most interested in all I had to tell him, and asked most pertinent questions about the passes and the supplies obtainable.

And so I returned for a time to ordinary regimental life. Of course, during my travels I had incurred considerable expenses for transport and this the Pay Department agreed to reimburse me. But first they required me to state the nature of the transport I had employed, and to submit receipts from the various people I had engaged. It gave me great pleasure to reply, "Carts of several kinds, ponies, mules, camels, yaks, boats, men and women; and that writing was an accomplishment unknown amongst Kashmiris, Gilgitis, Kirghiz, Tibetans, Ladakhis, etc". In the end they agreed to pay what I certified to be my actual out of pocket expenses.

The next episode was in 1895 in Chitral, south of Hunza and Nagar and facing Afghan Kafiristan. There was the customary dispute over succession which led to the usual murder of the Mehtar (prince) of Chitral. The usurper who took his place besieged the British representative in the fort at Chitral and managed to wipe out some small detachments on the road to Gilgit and Kashmir. The fort was gallantly held by Captain Townshend of the Central India Horse until a relieving force under Colonel Kelly arrived.

Later Townshend, as a General, commanded the Kut garrison in Mesopotamia in 1915.

CHAPTER VII

The Waziristan Delimitations Escort, 1894

For the next two years or so I settled down to normal regimental life and as I was the adjutant I was kept pretty busy. During this time the battalion took part in the Isazai Expedition in September–October 1892 which was a very short and easy affair – most noteworthy for the fact that there was a lot of sickness and cholera.

In 1894 I was appointed DAQMG to the Waziristan Delimitations Escort.

In November 1893 Sir Mortimer Durand, conferring with the Amir in Kabul, had arrived at an agreement regarding the demarcation of a boundary between Afghanistan and the independent tribes across the British border. This was supposed to be a peaceful mission and only a mixed brigade was detailed for the task. However, shortly after our arrival at Wana it was evident that the Mahsud Wazirs resented our presence. Before dawn 03NOV the Wana camp was rushed by some 1,500 Mahsuds – followers of that firebrand the Mullah Powindah. The brunt of the attack was borne by 1/1st Gurkha Rifles who behaved with great gallantry; the assailants were driven out of camp and then, pursued by the cavalry, suffered heavy losses.

An offence so grave could not be overlooked and a regular expedition of two divisions was mounted. It appeared that most of the maliks wanted peace but the turbulent mullah was too strong for them and so operations were put in hand. The mullah's village of Marobi was destroyed and before the end of December news came that the mullah had fled to Birmal. Whilst mopping up operations continued, the commander, Sir William Lockhart, continued with the demarcation mission which was duly completed.

After a brief interval with my battalion in Abbottabad in June 1895 I was ordered off to Chitral as brigade major of the first garrison to be stationed there. After a busy year there I went to England on furlo. Whilst on leave I got married but then hurried out to India again as I heard that the Tirah Expedition (see *Villiers-Stuart on the Frontier*) had been sanctioned and I was sure I would get employment with it. On the voyage out we had some distinguished passengers on board; General Sir William Lockhart who was to command the expedition, and Generals Lord Methven and Sir Ian Hamilton, both of whom were to be employed with the force. However on my way up country by train I was hauled off the train and ordered to report to Simla as DAAG at Army Headquarters.

This was doubly unfortunate for me as I missed the Tirah Expedition and then got grievously ill in Simla – and was invalided home to England. A nice start for my married life!

CHAPTER VIII

The China Expedition

On my return to India I became Private Secretary to the Lieutenant Governor of the Punjab which meant living in pleasant surroundings in Lahore and Simla. However I was warned that this soft post would do my career no good and within a few months I was appointed DAAG of the 2nd Brigade of the China Field Force, which was forming hurriedly for the relief of the Peking Legation.

Needless to say everyone wanted to take part in this expedition and the following officers of the regiment did so, E. B. C. Boddam, M. R. W. Nightingale and F. H. Bridges.

The 2nd Chinese War

There had been a dispute with China since 1856, the settlement of which had been held up by the Indian Mutiny. The real difficulty had been the old arrogant Chinese attitude which still refused to have any dealings with the 'outer barbarians' even though they had signed a treaty in 1858 agreeing to receive British and French ministers in Peking. When these ministers attempted to disembark at Taku in 1859 their landing was resisted, whereupon Admiral Hope attacked the Taku forts with seamen and marines. The landing party, hopelessly stuck in the mud, was beaten off with a loss of nearly half its strength. A bright spot in this rather ill-judged affair was the action of the American Commodore, Tatnall, who though officially a neutral, allowed his men to assist the British, observing, 'I guess blood is thicker than water'. The result was an expedition from India under Sir Hope Grant which, in conjunction with the French, arrived outside Peking in September 1860. So far there had been no serious fighting and the diplomats were busy settling matters with the Chinese on September 18th when the latter suddenly seized them and their

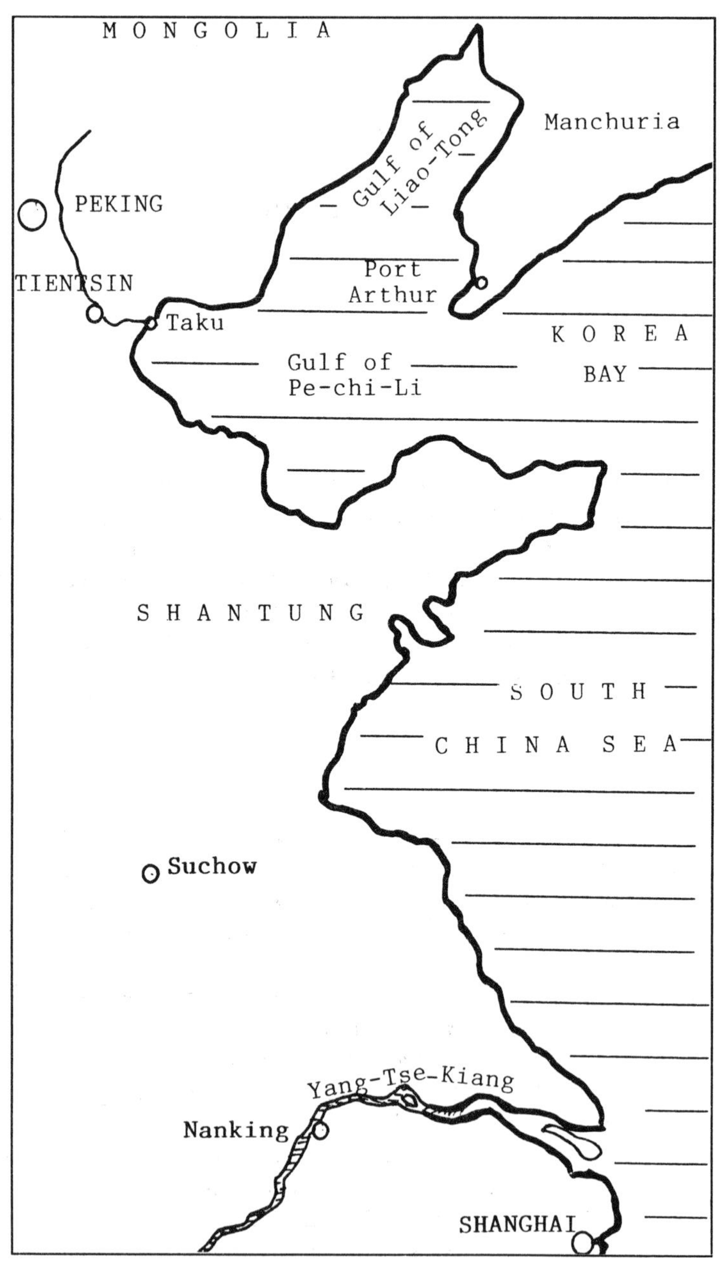
MONGOLIA
Manchuria
Gulf of Liao-Tong
PEKING
TIENTSIN
Port Arthur
Taku
KOREA BAY
Gulf of Pe-chi-Li
SHANTUNG
SOUTH CHINA SEA
Suchow
Yang-Tse-Kiang
Nanking
SHANGHAI

Map 8 — China.

escort and imprisoned them. The allies at once advanced on the city, whereon the survivors of their party were surrendered to them. They had been subjected to atrocious tortures from which half of them had perished. As a punishment for this iniquity the Summer Palace outside Peking was destroyed; a penalty which affected the Emperor himself and not only his subjects, who paid the increased war-indemnity. The port of Tientsin was opened to British trade and established the European right to trade in China.

The Boxer Rebellion 1900

In 1900 the Chinese hatred of the 'foreign devils' culminated in an anti-foreign rising instigated by a secret society whose euphonious title "The Harmonious Heavenly Fists" was rapidly abbreviated to "The Boxers"! Missionaries and their converts were murdered, the German Minister (von Ketteler) in Peking assassinated, and the foreign diplomats and residents shut up within the hastily fortified legation quarter, where with a scanty garrison they endeavoured to hold off the frenzied hordes without. The Dowager Empress, known as the 'Old Buddha' and the real ruler of China, did not officially countenance the rising, but she took no effective steps to suppress it. Eventually an international force gathered at Tientsin and, after one abortive advance, reached Peking in three weeks and relieved the legations, which it had been reported earlier had already fallen. British and Indian troops behaved gallantly in the advance and were the first to reach the legations, supported by Americans, French, Russians, Austrians, Italians, Germans and Japanese. By the end of the rebellion there was a total allied force of 50,000 of which 18,000 were British and Indian.

The British troops, which included a British naval brigade, had to bear the brunt of some hard fighting and sustained considerable casualties. The Royal Welsh Fusiliers were awarded the Battle Honour 'Peking' and 19 Indian Army regiments obtained the Battle Honour 'China'.

The Kaiser had managed to get a German general, Count von Wladersee, appointed as commander though, like most of the German troops, he did not arrive until the fighting was practically over. The Germans, however, distinguished themselves by carrying out their Kaiser's injunction to kill and slay "like the Huns of Attila" – an allusion familiar to German history and legend and inspired by fury at the death of von Ketteler; but destined to be taken up in the Great War in a manner very unacceptable to the principles of chivalry in war.

This had been a very interesting and exceptional experience, for in addition to seeing an absolutely new country, we met troops of nearly all nations. Our brigade, after many changes of plan, was detailed for Shanghai, and there we remained until the force was broken up.

I had a curious experience here. I had invited a French officer to dinner and among the diners was a French Canadian artillery officer, Major Boulanges, who arrived somewhat unexpectedly from South Africa. I had the French Canadian major on my right and the French officer on my left. I introduced them to each other and the French officer said, 'but you are French!' Boulanges said he certainly was. The French officer said, 'but how can that be, you are a major in the British artillery?' It took some time to clear up the situation. The French officer apparently had never realised the position of French Canadians. He also said, 'You talk the French of two centuries ago', to which Major Boulanges replied that that was about the time that his ancestors had emigrated to Canada.

In Shanghai we had a very strong and hand picked German regiment. Their officers were certainly a very charming lot and we were on the best of terms. We also had French troops and I had friendly relations with many of them. There were also a number of Russians, Japanese, Italians and Americans.

A strong brigade was to remain in China under my General, Sir O'Moore Creagh, VC, and he recommended that I stay with him as his senior staff officer; but the War Office decided that I, as a senior captain although I had the local rank of major, was too junior for the job. I and one or two others got a curious award, "Captain now Major to be Brevet Major" – not a very substantial distinction! A colonel was appointed in my place and I proceeded to England, travelling by Japan, Canada and New York; a most interesting and instructive journey. I travelled with my old CO, General Sir Alfred Gaselee, who had been commanding all the troops in China, and also some of his staff.

Japan was then, in 1901, not so developed as she has since become, and consequently still more attractive than now. Canada too, at that time, was not so opened up but we had a wonderful journey over the Rockies, across the prairies and the vast lakes to Toronto, Montreal, Quebec, and then down to New York where we embarked for England. Everywhere we had most friendly receptions.

I had about six months leave in England and then returned to India and back to regimental duties in 1902.

CHAPTER IX

Tibet

At the end of 1902 I was sent to a big concentration, manoeuvres and durbar at Delhi. I was DAAG of a brigade commanded by Sir James Willcocks, a well known general from whom I learned much. These manoeuvres were on a very large scale and the durbar was truly magnificent. The latter offered a marked contrast between the treatment of soldiers and civilians. We were on the lightest scale and British soldiers lay on the ground packed like sardines in quite small tents, and yet had to turn out spotlessly in full dress for ceremonial parades. Civilians had enormous tents splendidly furnished, and their camps beautifully laid out with electric light etc. We certainly suffered to make a Viceroy's holiday!

After a year or so with the Regiment I was appointed staff officer on the line of communications (L of C) of the Tibet Mission.

Incursions by Tibet into British Territory had been made, together with other slights. The Viceroy, Lord Curzon, now decided that strong action was necessary but initially the government decided to despatch only Colonel (afterwards Sir) F.E. Younghusband with a small escort to negotiate at Khambajong, to the north of the Sikkim frontier, The mission arrived there on 7th July 1903 where it remained until 11th December. No responsible Tibetan representatives appeared and such negotiations as were carried out were abortive. On 3rd October therefore the British Government authorised the occupation of the Chumbi valley and an advance to Gyantse. Military preparations, with the attendant problem of transport, were undertaken. Colonel Younghusband accompanied the mission which was commanded by General Ronald Macdonald. The Jelep La Pass was crossed and entry into Tibet effected on 12th December. An advance was made to Tuna, where part of the expedition wintered. A further advance being made on 31st March 1904, the

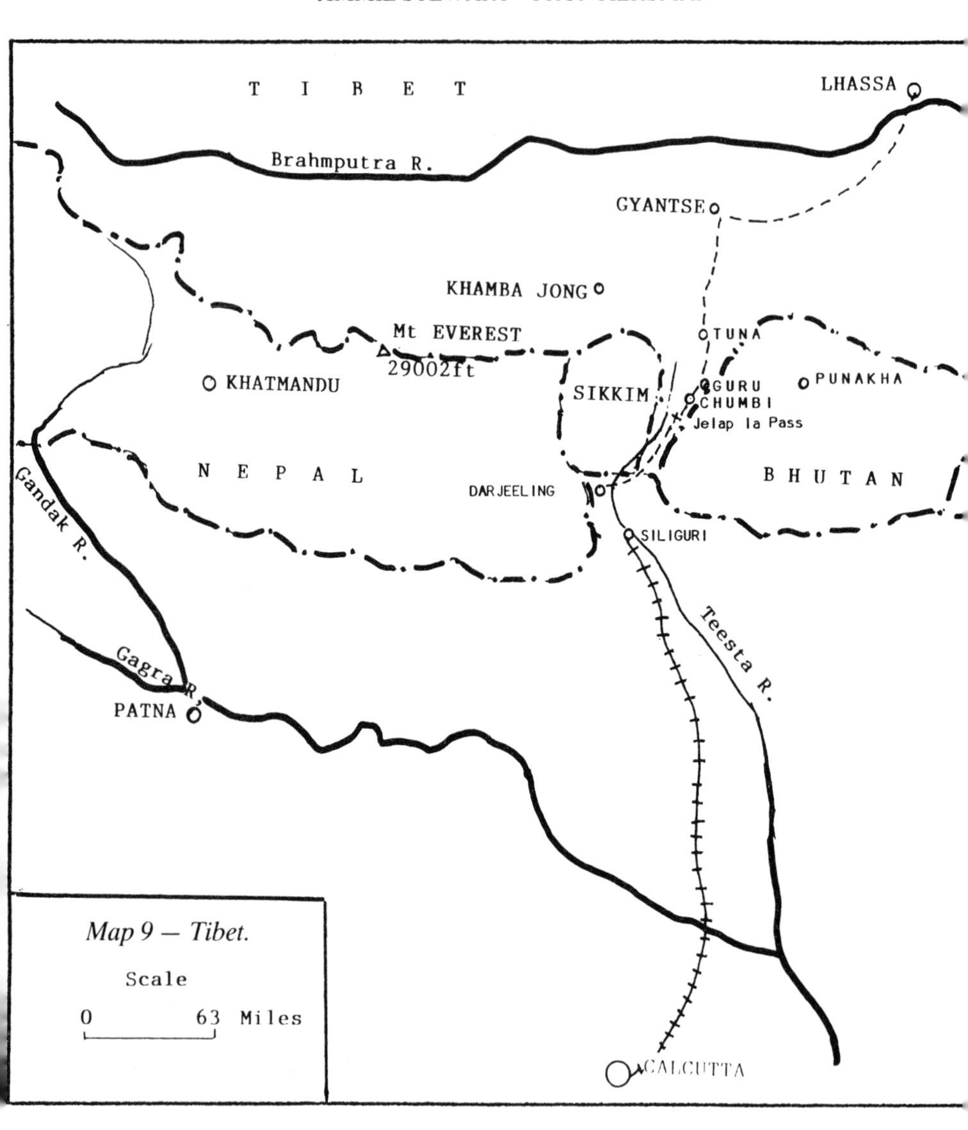
T I B E T
LHASSA
Brahmputra R.
GYANTSE
KHAMBA JONG
Mt EVEREST
29002ft
TUNA
KHATMANDU
SIKKIM
GURU
CHUMBI
Jelap la Pass
PUNAKHA
N E P A L
DARJEELING
B H U T A N
SILIGURI
Gandak R.
Teesta R.
Gagra R.
PATNA
CALCUTTA
Scale
0 63 Miles

Map 9 — Tibet.

first hostile encounter took place at Guru when the Tibetans (the aggressors) were defeated. With some further fighting en route the expedition reached and occupied Gyantse on 12th April. Here some of the British forces were beleaguered and the most serious fighting took place. In fact the advance to Lhasa, resumed after the storming of the Gyantse Jong (fort) on 6th July, met with comparatively little opposition and the capital was reached on 3rd August.

The L of C extended practically from Calcutta to Lhasa – many hundreds of miles – but we had little to do with the section from Calcutta to Railhead at Siliguri, at the foot of the Darjeeling hills. Our route from this point led through two channels; one over Darjeeling and down the Teesta valley, and the other along the Teesta river – a very hot and malarious region – whence it rose to the passes into Tibet; the Jelep La and the Nathu La (some 15,000ft) and so into the Chumbi valley. In bad weather these passes were very difficult; the troops suffering from high altitude and the accompanying mountain sickness.

HQ L of C was established at Chumbi, over 12,000ft but quite a pleasant spot with some shooting and fishing. But we had little time for anything but work. My general, Brigadier Hastings (uncle of General Sir Hastings Ismay) and I had to travel continuously, mostly towards Gyantse, which was to be the Advanced Base for the final march on Lhasa. There was very little fighting; an unnecessary scrap at Tuna, a night action at Gyantse, and a skirmish beyond that at Karo La – the highest elevation, I believe, in which troops were ever engaged – over 17,000ft.*

The great difficulty was getting up supplies. They were carried on every form of transport; elephants, camels, yaks, mules, ponies, donkeys and coolies of various nationalities, and even 'ekkas' – a two-wheeled bamboo cart brought from Calcutta, taken to pieces and carried over the passes by coolies. Put together again they were of great value on the high plains at 15,000ft between Phari and Gyantse. The physical and climatic conditions added greatly to our difficulties. Many men suffered temporarily from heart trouble, especially those carrying heavy loads. In nearly all cases chest expansion measurements went up considerably and health improved. Horses and ponies at first found difficulty in breathing and it was impossible to screw more than a walk out of them. Some of us tried to gallop down 'Kyangs' – wild asses – but our ordinarily faster animals came to a walk in no time. The rarity and dryness of the air and the low temperatures meant that our meat

---

Note* – In 1988 the Vir Chakra – Indian equivalent of the British VC – was awarded to a soldier of the Jammu Light Infantry for a patrol during operations in the area of the Siachen Glacier, at a height of over 21,000ft!

supplies kept indefinitely. Some Tibetans who were killed in the action near Tuna lay as they had fallen and seemed to undergo no change during the months I was in Tibet.

Owing to the piercing winds that blew during the day we moved mainly by night when it was comparatively still. But for days at a time I had to give up shaving as the water froze on my face as I tried to lather. I had very similar experiences on the Pamirs in 1891.

The Tibetans had a rather curious method of bathing. They hollowed out the trunk of a big tree, filled this with water and then dropped in a huge stone which had been heated in a nearby fire and on a sunny day this raised the temperature of the bath to a bearable heat. It was a rather public affair but no one of either sex seemed to mind.

My own experience did not extend beyond Gyantse as from there the columns which went on to Lhasa depended on what they could carry, supplemented by precarious local purchase. They had an anxious time, especially during the crossing of the Brahmaputra, but secured a completely successful end to the mission. I think all of us were glad to get back to normal altitudes and conditions.

The Dalai Lama had fled with his Russian friend Dorjiev. There was some delay in arranging a settlement due to the attitude of some of the lamas but finally a treaty of peace was concluded on 6th September.

The principle provisions of the Treaty were that the frontier of Sikkim was to be respected by the Tibetans; that markets for British trade would be established at Gyantse, Gartok and Yatung; that Tibet should pay an indemnity; that no foreign power, including the British, was to receive any concession in Tibet, territorial or mercantile, nor to concern itself in the government of the country.

The expedition left Lhasa on 23rd September, reaching India at the end of November. The Treaty, with slight modifications, was agreed by China on 27th April 1906.

The Anglo-Russian convention of 1907 determined the following conditions with respect to Tibet – the recognition of the souzerain rights of China and the territorial and administrative integrity of the country; that no official representative at Lhasa should be appointed either by England or by Russia, and that no concessions for railways, mines etc should be sought by either power.

With the 9th Gurkha Rifles

I rejoined the Regiment at the end of the year but in the New year of 1905 I was appointed to the 9th Gurkhas in Dehra Dun. They were being converted from Bengal Infantry into two battalions of Gurkhas, of which I was to command the 1st battalion. I superintended recruiting, training and even housing as we had to build our own barracks; but the officers and men were first class material so progress was easy and rapid. I had two years with them and then, owing to the sudden death of the CO of 2/5GR, I was transferred back to my own Regiment to replace him.

Whilst with the 9th Gurkhas I had two memorable experiences. I was detailed to go to Nepal to inspect the Resident's Escort in Khatmandu. Very few had been to Nepal in those days and so it was full of interest. Some of the journey was rather difficult, but when I reached the Khatmandu Valley I was met by a magnificent carriage-and-pair sent by the Maharajah. We drove at a great pace along the fine road for some six miles to the capital. This was a strange mixture of the old time Orient and the modern west. Beautiful temples and Nepalese buildings alongside a splendid electrically lit palace, and some very English looking houses. A very despotic 'Raj' rule, and a most cultured and charming Maharajah. He did everything to make my stay pleasant, even giving me the privilege of seeing a big parade of his own most efficient troops – the troops which he placed at our disposal during the Great War, when they did most valuable service.

The other event was a big concentration of troops at Agra in honour of the Amir of Afghanistan. The Viceroy, Lord Minto, and the C-in-C, Lord Kitchener, were both present, and I think the Amir must have been greatly impressed. It was certainly an excellent education for our newly raised 9th Gurkhas and I am confident that while learning much themselves, they gained considerable kudos from others.

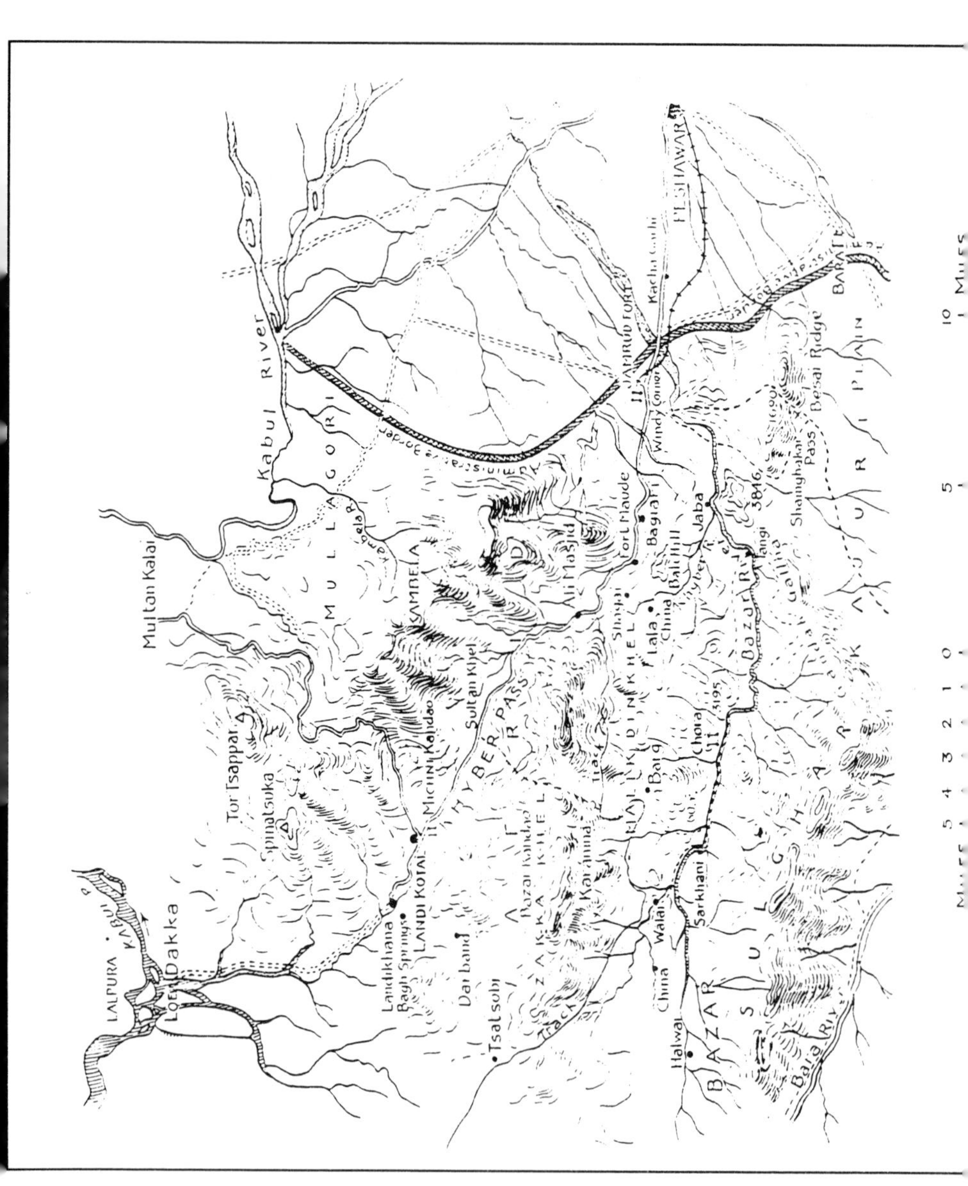

Map 10 — The Khyber Pass and Bazar Valley.

Major General Sir James M. Stewart, KCB CMG.
Colonel, 5th Royal Gurkha Rifles (Frontier Force).

Jimmie in 1866 – A Future Frontiersman.

Abbottabad in 1864.

Abbottabad 1920.

A Sergeant Bugler 1st Sikh Regiment (1880).

Quarterguard Commander 5th Gurkha Rifles (1896).

HQ 2nd Brigade leaves India for China. Capt. H.T. Brooking, Capt. J.M. Stewart (5GR), Capt. Gaisford, Capt. W.A. Watson, Lieut. Nightingale (5GR), Capt. F.C. Rampini, and sitting, General O'M. Creagh, VC (from The Times of India, *18th August 1900).*

Gyantse John (Fort) on the road to Lhasa.
(By permission of the Royal Geographical Society.)

Transport – Yaks harnessed to an Ekka.
(By permission of the Royal Geographical Society.)

View north of Hunza around Guimit and Pasu.
(Photo by A. B. P. Chadburn)

Another view to the north of Hunza.
(Photo by A. B. P. Chadburn)

Fertile valley of Hunza looking towards Nagar.

Baltoro Glacier where it runs into the Hunza River.
(Photo by A. B. P. Chadburn)

Lt. Col. J. M. Stewart
Commandant, 2/5 GR.

GOC Aden

Subadar Kishanbir Nagarkoti, IOM.

'Bullets' Subadar-Major Jangia Thapa.
(By permission of the National Army Museum)

The Regiment in Abbottabad, 1928.

Subadar Kishanbir Nagarkoti's medals

CHAPTER X

Willcocks's Weekend War
or
The Bazar Valley Expedition, 1908

It was very lucky for me that I did return to the 5th Gurkhas at this time for shortly afterwards 2/5th Gurkhas, which I was commanding, was detailed for the Zakka Khel Expedition under my old Chief, Sir James Willcocks.

The Tirah operations of 1897–1898 (see *Villiers-Stuart on the Frontier*) had led the Afridis to understand that their secluded villages and mountain fastnesses, nestling along the base of the Safed Koh, could no longer be regarded as inaccessible if the country was invaded by a determined and well-equipped force. The settlement concluded at the end of the operations proved satisfactory to both parties. The lenient and liberal terms granted by Government were appreciated by the tribesmen and as a result recruiting in the Indian Army and frontier militias became as brisk as ever. It may be confidently asserted that the stability of the peace would have been more permanent had it not been for the existence of certain sinister influences, which continually threaten to undermine the loyalty of the tribes to the British Government. The mullahs dwelling in tribal territory, as well as in Afghanistan are, by reason of their fanatical inclinations, ever prone to stir up strife against any alien government, while the presence of an anti-British party in Kabul affords a sure guarantee that disaffected tribes can obtain encouragement and support from that centre. In 1904 a large body of Afridis visited Kabul. They were well received and dismissed with substantial presents of cash and were allowed to purchase a number of rifles and ammunition. Aided and abetted by Kabul, the Zakka Khel who at this time could field a force of 6,000 armed riflemen, carried out a series of raids during the years 1904 to 1908, in spite of opposition from the remaining Afridis. On 28th January 1908 a daring enterprise against Peshawar city, when a policeman was killed and others wounded and property valued at one lakh of rupees was carried off to the hills, finally exhausted Government's patience.

It was decided to act, but restrictions were forced on the commander that operations would be against the Zakka Khel only. This tribe was based in the Bazar valley, the west end of which had two passes through which the tribesmen could retreat if necessary into Afghanistan. The action to be taken was to be promulgated to all the tribes at a Jirgah. It was considered imperative that an advance be made immediately after the Jirgah and that the operation would involve a flying column, to seal the exits at the west end of the valley whilst the main force advanced through the east end of the valley, which they would reach through the Chora Pass from Ali Masjid.

Meanwhile preparations were made for the secret mobilisation of two brigades and a reserve brigade, to be placed under the command of Major General Sir James Willcocks, KCMG CB DSO. On 2nd February the Force was warned to be ready to move at a moment's notice to take part in the Nowshera manoeuvres. On 4th February the warning order was followed by a definite order to mobilise for service on the frontier, followed by orders to entrain at 1400hrs on 6th February at Hasan Abdal. There was some delay while the Home and Indian Governments decided on the scope of the operations, and then orders came for the battalion to move to Peshawar where it arrived after dark on 11th February.

The Jirgah was held on 12th February and the remaining tribes fully agreed with the action being taken by the Government and promised their support for it. The two leading brigades of General Willcocks's force which now assembled at Peshawar were permitted to advance on the 13th.

General Willcocks's plans of campaign was to move the bulk of his force to Walai by the Chora Pass while sending a flying column under Colonel Roos-Keppel to carry out an encircling movement from Landi Kotal over the Bazar Pass to China. The flying column was to consist of 300 Rifles of 2/5GR and 800 Rifles of the Khyber Rifles, and was ordered to assemble at Landi Kotal.

On 13FEB, a fine and bright day typical of the cold weather of northern India, the well-worn road from Peshawar was once again the stage for scenes so often enacted there before, as the two brigades of the main column streamed along it towards the Khyber to the music of the regimental bands and the skirl of the Pipes, while seemingly endless streams of camels and mules raised clouds of dust in their rear. That night was spent in camp at Jamrud and next day the force marched to Lala China, just short of Ali Masjid in the Khyber. On 15th February active operations began.

For the entry into the Bazar Valley the Commander had arranged that, simultaneously with the advance of the flying column from Landi Kotal, 2 Brigade, equipped as lightly as possible, should move ahead by the Chora Pass and, securing the main features of the Zakka Khel portion of the route, should make for the neighbourhood of Walai. 2/5GR (less the flying column detachment) was attached to 2 bde and, extricating itself with some difficulty from the broken ground on which it was bivouacked, set off at dawn with three days' haversack rations and only 7lb of bedding for the men. From Lala China to Chora, with its white fort set imposingly on the left bank of the Bazar stream, is a distance of seven miles and on this part of the route, traversing as it does the country of the friendly Malik Din Khel, no opposition was met. About a mile west of Chora the track enters Zakka Khel country, and here it is commanded by the lofty ridge known as Tsapara, rising above the left bank of the stream.

The advanced guard reached this point at midday and at once came under fire from a body of the enemy posted on the slopes of the ridge. The advance of the column was checked and during this short pause I received a message telling me to clear the Tsapara ridge and to hold it during the night with the aim of securing communication with Chora.

The battalion advanced rapidly up parallel spurs and, driving the enemy before them were soon in possession of the crest. The only casualties were among the mules of the Machine Gun (MMG) section and first line transport which had been sent to shelter in a deep nullah near the foot of the ridge and came under fire from enemy retiring from the ridge. Consolidation of the ridge took place and during the night a bold attack was made on the position by the Zakka Khel. The first indication was a heavy burst of firing from some high ground and soon the sentries, who happened to be two tough old soldiers, passed the word that the enemy were close at hand. Word was passed from man to man and in a moment everyone was on the alert, ready to repel a rush. Some thirty yards from a sangar, enemy were seen creeping up under the cover of the fire from the high ground, and soon they too opened fire on the sangar. Firing continued till dawn when the enemy withdrew leaving three dead. We suffered no casualties other than three more mules.

To complete the events of 15FEB, the remainder of 2 bde had bivouacked near Walai and 1 bde, with the baggage columns had halted for the night at Chora.

On 16FEB 28th Punjabis arrived to take over the Tsapara ridge positions and 2/5GR, having sent its mules down to complete the journey by road, set out on a long stiff climb over the hills to Walai. Whilst this move was in progress considerable numbers of the enemy were seen to our front who appeared to be hotly engaging some of our own troops who were trying to make their way up the hill from the valley below. I decided to lend a hand and began a turning movement which would bring the battalion out on the hills overlooking the enemy position. All went well until we arrived at that position, when it came under heavy MMG fire from the battalion which we were trying to assist, thinking that we were Afridis. We were obliged to move below the cover of the ridge and continue with our advance to Walai.

On arrival there we met Major Lucas with the flying column detachment of 2/5GR, which had left Landi Kotal at 0400hrs on 15FEB to arrive at China the same day by way of the Bazar Pass after a very hard march. Having spent the day at China, where the enemy snipers had been busy, they had come on to join 2 bde at Walai on 16FEB.

Walai had been selected as the standing camp for the force, though it was in fact a bivouac camp with no tents and merely the point from where parties would be sent out daily to harry the enemy. In this part of the Bazar valley there are two main branches of the Bazar stream, which run nearly parallel and about two miles apart, to unite at a point 1500yds south-east of Walai. It was overlooked on the west and south by the Khar Ghundai feature, known also as Seaforths' Hill, situated between the two branches, and by a spur running down from Sara Paial, named 45th Sikhs Hill, which rose above the right bank of the southern branch. On the north and east the camp was commanded by the Zir Ghundai feature and by a range of low hills which curved towards the junction of the streams. All these features were strongly piquetted and an inner line of defence was provided by a breastwork built round the camping ground.

The night 16/17FEB, like most nights at Walai, was disturbed by enemy sniper fire. On 17FEB 1 bde moved in from Chora and 2/5GR was sent across the nullah to join them and take over part of their perimeter in the north west area of the camp. The men set to work at digging what is expressively known as 'funk holes'. Men of other regiments in the brigade stood around and smiled at this display of energy, for they had found Chora quiet enough but a night spent without cover at Walai taught them wisdom and they were quick to follow our example.

China, a few miles west of Walai, a place of many towers, springs of good water, of fruit trees and fertile fields, is the only settlement of real importance in the valley, and against it the initial efforts of the expedition were directed. On 18FEB 2/5GR formed part of a mixed force under General Barrett for the destruction and capture of China. Leaving camp before daylight 2/5GR and the Seaforths made a slight detour to bring them onto the low ridge half encircling China from the north, while the rest of the force moved straight at China. On approaching our ridge we met some opposition, but advancing rapidly 2/5GR soon reached the crest of the ridge; the enemy withdrew towards Tsatsobi and Thabai. We consolidated our position to hold it for the day. Meanwhile the rest of the force had reached China from the east and the work of blowing up towers, collecting firewood and fodder and destroying the fruit trees and water supply began. Retirement to Walai began at 1600hrs and as usual the enemy collected magically from nowhere and attempted to follow up. The pace of the battalion and the excellence of its layback and covering fire arrangements were effective in keeping them at a distance, but on the other flank they succeeded in getting close to No. 3 Mtn Bty in fairly open country and they and their escort from 54th Sikhs were hotly engaged for a time. However 54th Sikhs drove off the enemy and by 1800hrs the whole force was within the shelter of the camp piquets. The enemy, which had lost heavily, appeared to have had their fill for the day and we had a quiet night without one shot being fired.

Operations continued in the area and though the enemy tried to interfere they met with no success.

On 20FEB four companies of 2/5GR were available for operations, the remainder being used up on camp piquet duties, and we were detailed to accompany a column detailed for the destruction of Sarmando and Khwar, followed by a reconnaissance towards the Tsatsobi Pass. There was ineffective long range sniping and the column returned to camp having accomplished its mission.

Operations on 21FEB were on a larger scale, both brigades being employed. For some days past the enemy had been assembling in considerable numbers at Halwai, six miles west of Walai, and general Willcocks seized the opportunity to attack them and destroy the village. 2 bde moved south of China leaving 28th Punjabis en route in occupation of China Hill to cover the subsequent withdrawal of the force, and sending the Seaforths to hold a position on the hills south-east of Walai. 2/5GR, working with 1 bde moved north of China and crossing the Sarwakai Pass, advanced southwards across the plain to attack frontally the Halwai position. Moving with great speed 2/5GR soon gained possession of the hills and inflicted a number of casualties on the retiring enemy. The towers of Halwai were destroyed, stacks of timber burned, and then the withdrawal was started. Both bdes took the line south of China and for a time all went well. However parties of the enemy had been able to approach close to 28th Punjabis on China Hill and when they began their withdrawal they came under heavy fire, delivered from the crest at close range, and suffered some casualties. Emboldened by this success they pressed hard on the heels of the Seaforths withdrawal through the plain to the south, when one officer was killed.

On 23FEB the battalion paid another visit to China and then next day was employed on convoy duty towards Chora. A large Jirgah of Afridis arrived in camp and offered to negotiate with the Zakka Khels, and so hostilities were postponed for two days.

It was in this period when Sir James Willcocks had an amusing encounter with one of our men. Meeting the rifleman one morning when taking a letter to the post the rifleman saluted smartly and said, 'are you the biggest General Sahib here?'

'I am,' said the general.

'Then will you post this letter for me?'

'But why not take it to the Field Post Office yourself?'

'It is a very important letter to my wife in Abbottabad; I do not trust the Field Post Office because it does not use stamps. But if the big General Sahib will send my letter with his own, it will without doubt arrive.'

Sir James good naturedly took the letter and posted it.

The Afridi Jirgah had gone to Halwai on 25FEB and returned on 28FEB to say that the Zakka Khels had agreed to the terms. On 29FEB the camp broke up and, the battalion acting as rear guard, the force withdrew.

The operation was completed with such success and so quickly that it became known as 'Willcocks's Weekend War'. Testimony to the success of the expedition from the enemy side is given in the 'Political Report of the Bazar Valley Expedition 1908'.

"The Afridis, who are no mean judges of hill fighting, express themselves amazed at the handling and conduct of the troops as unlike anything they have seen or heard of, and the fact that they have obtained no loot in mules, rifles, stores or ammunition, on which they confidently counted to compensate them for their losses, has given them a strong distaste for expeditions conducted on these novel lines."

The battalion had borne itself in accordance with the traditions of the Regiment. I was promoted to a brevet colonelcy and appointed ADC to the King.

CHAPTER XI

The Last Days of Peace

We had only just returned to Abbottabad from the Bazar Valley when fresh trouble broke out on the Peshawar border with the Mohmand tribes and an expedition was mounted. We were held in reserve at Kala-ki-Serai but we were not required. We were there in May and June – the hottest months – and as we were in tents it was rather a trying time.

Cavalry Charge

In the cold weather of that year, 1908–1909, there were large manoeuvres held south of Rawalpindi, in which I acted as brigadier. My main recollection was that of surprising a British cavalry regiment at dawn – they had not taken adequate precautions.

I spent that summer in England and on returning to the Regiment we went off on manoeuvres again. This time the same British cavalry Regiment gave me and the Regiment a big surprise. It was considered advisable to give Gurkhas – all hillmen – the experience of a cavalry charge. It proved most realistic. The cavalry charged right through us, but the men stood absolutely still. I and the adjutant, in much trepidation, followed their example, and our steadiness proved our salvation.

Early in 1910 I was appointed to officiate as Deputy Secretary in the Army Department; a curious appointment, for it meant scrutinising all the most important military proposals before they were submitted to the Government of India. The Chief Secretary was Sir Robert Scallon, a most able and rapid worker, but he liked me to settle all I could and only submit to him the biggest cases. I learned much and, I regret to say, saw how jealous high up men could be. As a young officer I had always imagined that commanders all worked together loyally in support of their chief. I was disillusioned. I had heard rumours that in the Home Army senior officers – to use polo phraseology – were given to riding each other off. I now saw that in India they had not learned to play the game.

I took over the appointment in Calcutta, and it meant a busy time professionally and socially. Lots of work and lots of play, but it all centred around the 'Maidan', a very large grass plain bordering on the Hughli River. I lived in the Bengal Club, a marble palace, on one side of the Maidan, while my office was on the far side. I used to ride on the race course every morning, and I played or watched tennis and cricket, and even football, in the evenings. I frequently visited and dined in the Fort overlooking the Hughli where the C-in-C and many senior officers lived and where a British battalion was stationed.

When the hot weather came we moved to Simla, where I was on familiar ground. Work was hard and my working day was normally twelve hours. But exercise kept me fit.

Returning to the Regiment in the autumn I spent much of the time on cold weather manoeuvres, which were certainly the dustiest that I can remember.

Coronation Duties

After the Zakka Khel Expedition of 1910 I had been appointed ADC to the King and now, in May 1911, I and other ADCs were ordered home with a large Indian army contingent to take part in the Coronation ceremonies. We travelled in a special ship and had a very enjoyable voyage.

We ADCs from India had an especially good time. 'Birdie', (afterwards FM Sir William Birdwood), was one of our number and he was on the Staff of Lord Kitchener, who was in command of all the troops at the Coronation. He secured for us exceptional treatment as regards riding in processions, seats at the Abbey, lunch at the Guildhall, tickets for the Royal Enclosure at Ascot and other functions. I rode in two processions. In the first I was given a very nice looking mare to ride and I was told that she had jumped at Olympia. I said I did not want a horse for jumping, but they guaranteed that she would stand anything, and so she did, colours lowered almost under her nose, flags waved in her face, cheering crowds etc. But she never walked from start to finish and her restiveness caused some anxiety to a noble duke riding near me.

That evening Charles Mellis VC (later Sir Charles Mellis) and I went to the Empire to see a film of the procession, early days of films, but as we arrived just too late to see ourselves ride by, we were very disappointed.

In the second procession I got a less showy and very steady horse, which had been ridden in the previous procession and recommended by my old friend Henry Stanton (later Sir Henry Stanton). On this occasion we trotted from Buckingham

Palace to the Guildhall, where the King lunched with the Lord Mayor, and we had a gorgeous meal at a table reserved for the Royal Household. After lunch we rode at a walk through north London, but on reaching the Marble Arch we trotted all the way home to Buckingham Palace.

London was very full and accommodation very difficult to procure, but we eventually got rooms at the St Ermine's Hotel, Westminster, not far from the Abbey. To get to the Abbey I hired a splendid carriage-and-pair and drove there in state. For the actual Coronation Service my wife and I were given seats in the Abbey, very high up but with a good view of the proceedings. On coming out of the Abbey there was no sign of our carriage so we walked back to the hotel. There were no motors in those days and it was a glorious day, so we did not mind the inconvenience.

After the Coronation I took leave in England and as my tenure of command in the Regiment was over I was unemployed – but not for long as my old Chief, Sir Robert Scallon, who had been appointed to command the Burma Division, applied for me as his senior Staff Officer and AQMG. I took up this appointment in April 1912.

Burma

It was very interesting to see Burma again after a gap of twenty-three years. The country had certainly advanced, but in the towns the manners of the people had not been improved by increased education. In the country districts the Burmese were the same happy, courteous folk, delightful to meet but difficult to work with. Burma does not lend itself to soldiering on a large scale; the climate, the nature of the country and the necessary distribution of the troops are all against it, but we managed somehow to have some camps and manoeuvres, and I travelled extensively on inspection work.

My most interesting trips were to the Chinese frontier beyond Mykitna; the Chin Hills which I had seen opened up in 1889; and to the Andaman islands – a vast convict settlement where there were some 1400 prisoners – the larger proportion of which were murderers for whom extenuating circumstances had been found to prevent their execution, men like trans-border Pathans who had to carry out blood feuds, and Burmese who always carry dahs (swords) and use them in the heat of the moment. Nearly all the servants of the officials were murderers. They were considered to be the most trustworthy and reliable, and far more preferable to the thieves, coiners, etc.

I made friends with a trans-border man, a Mohmand, when he found I could talk his language and give him news of the north-west frontier. His luck had been out when he had killed his enemy inside our border and had been caught before he could escape to his own territory, where he would have gained much honour for his deed.

I had three months leave in England at the end of 1913 and then returned to routine work until July 1914, when I was detailed to attend a staff conference in Simla. The atmosphere was very tense then and as we left Calcutta at the end of the month for our return to Rangoon, we arranged to have a marconigram sent to us if war broke out. On arrival in Rangoon we found that war preparations had started and I went around all the forts and defences on inspection before going on to HQ at Maymyo.

On 10AUG I received orders to go to Calcutta at once for overseas duty. I had no idea whether I was destined for France, Egypt, Africa or Vladivostock, so I must be prepared for the tropics or the Arctic regions.

At Calcutta I found elaborate arrangements had been made to rush me across India to Karachi where secret orders would await me. At Karachi I was met by a senior staff officer who handed me orders which were to be opened when I had got on board and then I must communicate them to the Commander of the vessel. Everybody I met told me the 69th Punjabis were already on board and that we were bound for East Africa. The Commander also knew this and told me he had taken on all the necessary coal and provisions. When I opened my secret orders they confirmed what everyone already knew!

CHAPTER XII

East Africa

We sailed on 19th August 1914 and I believe we were the first troops to leave India that year for active service overseas. We had an uneventful voyage, unescorted as far as the equator, where we were met by *HMS Fox*, which was to protect our voyage to Mombasa. Mercifully we were not intercepted by the *Koenigsberg* for I understand she would probably have sunk us on sight.

Our boat was very old and ill-equipped, though the officers did all they could for us. So when the Captain of the *Fox* sent me a cipher message in the middle of the night asking me, if I was junior in rank to him, to come on board and have breakfast, I replied that though I was years senior to him I would gladly waive ceremony and go on board, where I hoped to have a really good meal.

The Captain was rather a strange fellow. He assured me that he was fully acquainted with the situation in East Africa, that there was no urgency about our arrival, and that he proposed to use our transport to tow targets for his gun practices. His appreciation of the situation proved very incorrect, for on landing at Mombasa on 1st September, I found affairs were in a critical position. The Germans were reported to be threatening the Uganda railway by various small advances and our Intelligence service, though rapidly improving, was rather vague. This railway was the crucial point in the defence of British East Africa, so I realised at once that to safeguard it was our first concern.

I was fortunate in having Colonel L.E.S. Ward, formerly of the Oxfordshire LI, to advise me. He had been an officer in the King's African Rifles (KAR) and then a settler in Uganda. With the small forces at his disposal he had already started the organisation of the defence. And these forces were very small. Some companies of the KAR – first class men with exceptionally good British officers – a couple of hundred or so of the East African Mounted Rifles (EAMR), a small detachment of

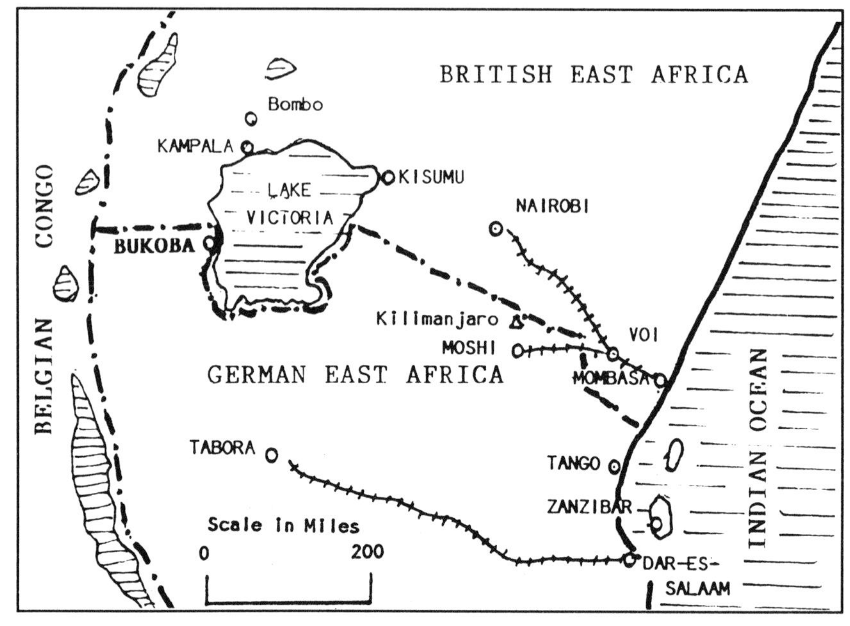

Map 11 — East Africa.

volunteers in Mombasa, and a unit of Indian railway workers hastily raised for the defence of the railway. Artillery there was none. It was evident that there was no regular pre-war scheme for the defence of the colony.

The Germans were in a much better position. They had artillery, and they had a strong foundation of well trained ex-officers and men from the Germany army, and some capable commanders.

We were lucky in having in the EAMR a number of ex-officers of our own Navy and Army, mostly British cavalry, and some very useful civilians, including a good many Dutch. These were practically all settlers, used to East Africa and its inhabitants. These settlers had certainly played up wonderfully, and had put their country well before their private interests. The officials, too, whenever they could be spared were employed in ancillary services; medical, sanitary, transport, etc. Much, of course, remained to be done, but the foundations had been laid quite efficiently.

Still, the railway was the primary consideration. I arranged for half a battalion of the 29th Punjabis to leave at once for Voi, which seemed to be the most vital point. Within a very short time of their arrival they, in conjunction with some of the KAR, were in conflict with a German force which had reached within a few miles of the railway. The Germans had a disagreeable surprise. Evidently they had not expected any reinforcements from India.

I myself proceeded to Nairobi, the capital of the colony, to get in touch with the whole situation, and to complete all organisations as far as possible.

I do not propose to go into the detail of the military developments of the next few months. They consisted mainly in a series of small encounters with German detachments who were endeavouring to seize or destroy points on the railway. I will give you one typical example of such encounters.

A small patrol of EAMR, moving in very thick thorn bush, was surprised by a German detachment. They had several casualties among the men and animals, and two badly wounded men could not be got away. The Germans also could not move them, but they tied white clothes in some trees nearby to assist their discovery. These men lay out all night, and had to listen to lions devouring some of the mules which had fallen near them. They themselves were not molested, and were brought in by some of our men in the morning, and ultimately recovered their health and, I believe, their nerve.

The railway itself, the good information provided by our Intelligence service, and the efficiency of our own troops enabled us to frustrate all the enemy endeavours. The Governor, Sir Henry Belfield, subsequently paid me the compliment of saying that while I was in command we had known nothing but success, and I like to think that this was so.

I certainly had a very busy time. I had to get to know the country, the people and the conditions generally. I travelled continuously between Mombasa and Kisumu on the Victoria Nyanza, and even across to Uganda, and to outlying posts, as long as I could maintain touch.

But I was not to remain in chief command for long. Originally I had been given the command of Force 'C', organised in India for the defence of British East Africa, and on 2nd September I had been promoted to Brigadier-General. This force consisted largely of Imperial Service Troops of very varying value, but stiffened by some good regular units. To carry out the invasion of German East Africa, India organised Force 'D', a considerably larger force but composed also of many units that would not ordinarily have been employed against a formidable enemy. India had seriously underestimated the value of the equipment, armament and personnel of the Germans in East Africa. This Force 'D' was under the command of Brigadier-General A.E. Aitken, with three brigadiers under him, Wapshare, Tighe and Malleson. I had been able to send India accurate reports of the opposition they were likely to meet, but India and the India Office knew better.

CHAPTER XIII

ATTACK ON GERMAN EAST AFRICA

It was decided that in 1915 we would capture German East Africa (later Tanganyika), where the enemy forces were commanded by a brilliant German officer, Colonel von Lettow-Vorbeck.

I went down to Mombasa at the end of October and met General Aitken and most of his Staff. They had landed there to confer with me, while the transports with his troops remained at sea. We settled plans; he to attack Tanga in German East Africa, while I co-operated in British East Africa, by demonstrations along the coast and from Voi, and an advance on Longidu. We carried out our part of the programme, and waited to hear of the success of Force 'D', but waited in vain. The news we got was that they had been repulsed and were coming in to Mombasa. I will not criticise the whole action. Many of us who knew India had anticipated that the troops detailed were not good enough, but this was further complicated by a want of secrecy about their intentions, undue confidence and a lack of determination.

The failure of the British landing at Tanga in November 1915 with 800 casualties had demonstrated the difficulties to be encountered in the conquest of Germany's last remaining colony. When the war began Colonel von Lettow-Vorbeck had less than 5000 men under arms, including a few hundred Europeans. Later however, by utilising every conceivable resource, he brought into the field at various times nearly 4000 Europeans and over 20,000 warlike 'Askaris'. The East African campaign was therefore a serious matter and the problem was increased by the incredibly difficult nature of the country where thick bush, particularly in the south, gave every advantage to the defending force. In April 1915 a blockade runner reached the coast and, though sunk, the Germans managed to salvage the arms and ammunition she carried.

With the arrival of Force 'D' in British East Africa and all the consequent redistributions, I lost my independent command, as the chief command was taken over temporarily by General Aitken. He was succeeded at the beginning of December by General Wapshare, while General Tighe and I commanded the two areas into which BEA was divided – Mombasa and Nairobi respectively.

I have an entry dated 9th December in the small personal diary which I then kept:-

> "As I used to run the whole show with ease, alone, it seems to me we have a plurality of Generals, and that I am superfluous, but I couldn't persuade them. I made several attempts to get transferred to some other sphere of operations, and I believe that General Wapshare did eventually represent my views, but nothing resulted. I was told in about 1932 by an officer on General Maude's Staff in Mesopotamia that he himself had actually sent off a telegram from General Maude, asking for me as his Chief of Staff, but India had refused – said I could not be spared. So we settle down to a rather pacific attitude, waiting for reinforcements to commence a really active campaign."

In January 1915 I had an interesting trip to Victoria Nyanza, including a small action at Shirati, where we took and destroyed a German fort; and a tour along the Kagera river, where our posts were in close contact with the German ones and brushes were frequent.

In February I had another trip on the lake and had a look at the German position at Bukoba, with a view to possible future action; and then I visited Entebbe, getting more fully in touch with the local situation.

In April General Wapshare was transferred and General Tighe assumed the command in BEA; General Malleson taking over the Mombasa area while I retained the Nairobi District. We lived in hope of additional troops being sent to us, which would enable us to invade German East Africa. Meanwhile we were busy in making all possible preparations for such an advance. I did a lot of travelling, inspecting and organising. The hospital arrangements and raising of transport units required special attention.

The Germans continued their attempts to blow up the railway, and I know a train I was in on one occasion had a narrow escape, but on the whole we got off without any serious loss.

At the end of April I made another tour in the Victoria Nyanza area, and again had a look at the Bukoba position and even exchanged a few shots with the garrison there.

In May I had to inspect a newly arrived battalion, the 25th Bn (Legion of Frontiersmen) of the Royal Fusiliers – a most interesting and unique unit. They were well over a thousand strong, but more than half of them had never fired a rifle and a large portion had never seen a frontier, while many were well beyond the normal military age. But there was a strong leaven of first class material, and a very fine spirit. Practically all the officers had seen service and many were experienced sportsmen. They were commanded by Colonel Driscoll who had made a name for himself in the South African campaign, and under him were such well known hunters as Selous, Outram and Cherry Kearton, and several ex-officers of the British Service. One junior officer had been a Major-General in the Honduras Army; one in the French Foreign Legion; and one told me he had lived by promoting revolutions in South America! In the ranks there was a somewhat similar element, and a strong sprinkling of old soldiers and sailors who had been rejected for home service on account of age, but were passed fit for work in the wilds and climate of East Africa! I was told they could provide a representative of every trade and profession, and all the personnel of a murder trial except for the corpse. But their keenness made up for all shortcomings and they did fine service under me, and later on in German East Africa.

During our more inactive periods I had quite a pleasant time socially, some enjoyable hunting, we ran anything from lions to jackals and even porcupine, tennis, cricket, squash, polo of a kind, and dinners galore. On my various tours we saw and occasionally got any amount of game, lions (I never got one), harte-beest, wildebeest, gazelle, deer, antelope, rhino, hippo and guineafowl, bustard and other birds.

Bukoba

In June I was given command of a column to attack the German position at Bukoba. The column, a very useful little force, consisted of strong detachments from the Loyal North Lancs, the 15th battalion the Royal Fusiliers, the 29th Punjabis, the 3rd KAR, some Maxims from the EAMR and a section of the 28th Indian Mountain Battery. They all embarked on the 19th and 20th June on the various ships we had on the Lake; the *Winifred*, the *Rusinga*, the *Usoga* and the *Nyanza*, and some smaller craft. On my previous trips on the lake I had reconnoitred Bukoba, and had made up my mind as to the best method of attack.

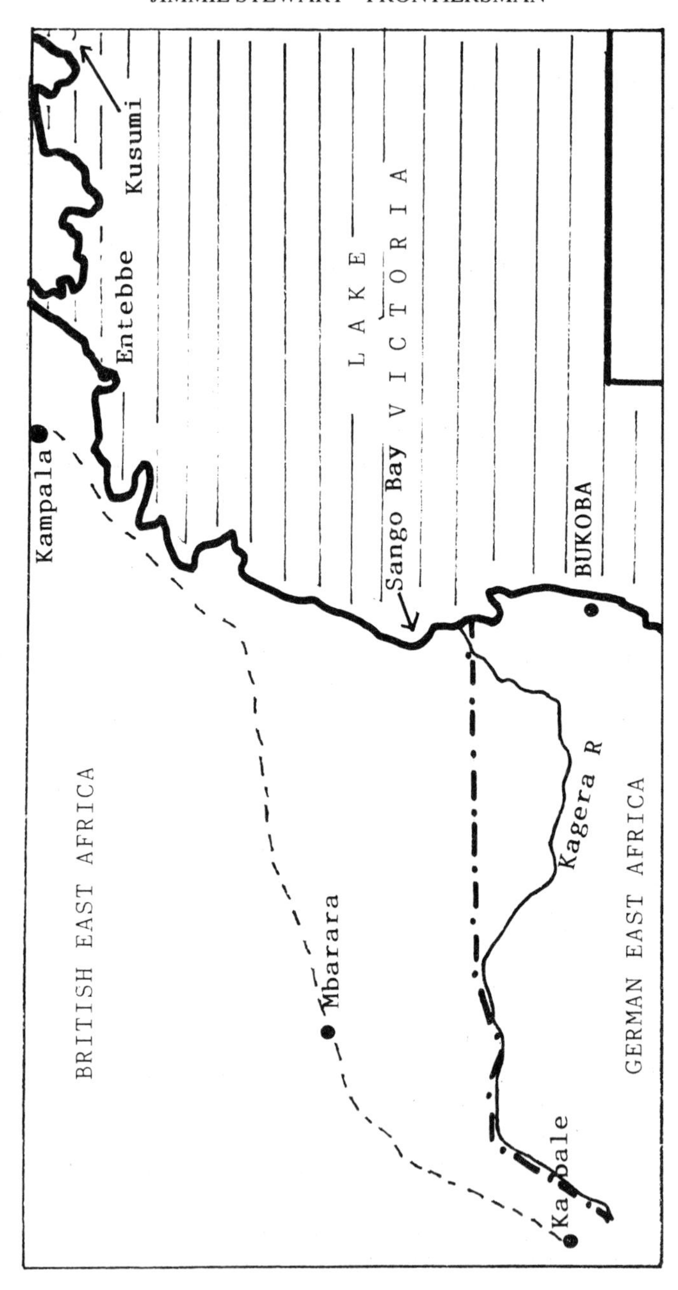

Map 12 — Bukoba.

We got near Bukoba, with all our lights out, about midnight or the 21st June, but were heard by a German outpost on a small island which sent up warning rockets and lit flares. My plan was to demonstrate strongly in front of Bukoba and at dawn to land our main force about three miles away behind a hill, which screened our movements completely. All went well. There was some exchange of artillery fire in front of Bukoba, but our main force got ashore unopposed and soon secured their position. We then advanced against Bukoba, driving the Germans from the advanced posts, with the guns on our ships in front of Bukoba protecting our left flank, and established ourselves on some hills near Bukoba before nightfall. The next morning we continued our advance and were soon in possession of Bukoba, where we destroyed the fort and their important wireless station, captured the German flag* and secured a considerable amount of ammunition and stores, and a large collection of ivory tusks; and then, in accordance with our instructions, re-embarked, without any real interference from the enemy.

As far as I could tell everything had gone without a hitch, and the whole operation had been completely successful. This was all the more satisfactory as it was the first considerable success we had secured in East Africa. We were given quite a reception when we got back to Nairobi, but far more important, I got a telegram of congratulations from Lord Kitchener, and soon after was specially promoted Major-General.

The next two months I spent mainly in touring, training and inspecting troops, but in September I had a very interesting time. I was detailed to establish communications with the Belgian forces in the upper reaches of the Congo, and to arrange for their co-operation when we advanced into German East Africa. I visited Uganda first, staying at Entebbe and from there went to Kampala and on to Bombo – the Headquarters of the 4th King's African Rifles (4/KAR) – and then returned to Entebbe. An interesting and useful little tour over good roads through attractive country with pleasing inhabitants. I then crossed the Victoria Nyanza to Sango Bay and proceeded up the Kagera, visiting our various posts vis-à-vis the German outposts, which were plainly visible and with which our men had occasional encounters.

I was very struck by the excellent arrangements at all our posts by the various officers, regulars, police and civilians, and they all seemed to enjoy their remote but very active lives. For several marches we were right away from the roads and it

---

Note* – This flag was captured by the Royal Fusiliers, and was given to General Stewart, and since his death it has been returned to that regiment.

meant riding through all sorts of country; hills, plains, swamps, forests and sometimes walking through tse-tse fly areas. We saw lots of game and tracks of elephants and buffalo.

We had one most disagreeable experience. We were caught in a very violent storm with torrents of rain and continuous thunder and lightning. We took refuge in a hut with our ponies. There was a sudden crash and two or three of my staff collapsed. The lightning had struck quite close, run along the wet ground and brought them down, but they soon recovered.

Our cars had to follow different routes, but managed to join us at various stages. Much of the road had to be repaired, much had to be made and many light bridges had to be improved. Our route took us where cars had never penetrated and they had narrow escapes from complete wreckage.

We were wonderfully received everywhere, villagers sometimes lining the roads, kneeling as we passed and greeting us by clapping their hands and strange cheers. The chiefs too were very friendly and anxious to help in every way. Evidently this was due to the influence of our district officers and missionaries of various denominations. This latter influence in some cases did not prevent a plurality of wives. One magnificent chief, standing about 6ft 6ins, had a dozen or so and we were told they received no marks of royal favour until they had been fattened for some months on a milk diet. At one place, Mbarara, we were even met by a guard of honour of African boy scouts who treated me to a 'General salute'.

At Kabale I was met by Colonel Henri and several Belgian officers. They all seemed delighted to see us and assured us of their willingness to co-operate in due course. All their arrangements appeared to be efficient and their Askaris a very useful lot. We spent three days with them, crossed a large lake in canoes to Engazi and to a high point where we got a magnificent view of Lake Mulera (in German hands), of the Kigewzi valley and of some hills where 'Three Empires Meet' – British, Belgian and German. We then commenced our return journey by more or less the same route, and got back to Nairobi by the end of the month.

We now began to receive small reinforcements, but not sufficient to justify any advance into German East Africa (GEA), but were buoyed up with hopes of more reinforcements to follow.

Two senior Dutch officers (now referred to as South Africans since the Boer war) came up from South Africa to learn about our situation and it fell to me to take them around. I was struck by the very indifferent view they took of the African and Indian soldiers. To them they were just 'niggers' or 'coolies'. In the first serious encounter in which the South Africans were engaged, they learned how reliable these coloured troops could be, and were only too glad to receive their support!

Among the first reinforcements to reach us was a really fine Rhodesian regiment; all settlers or officials with excellent officers and first class men. With this prospect of an early advance we arranged a fresh deployment of our force, and I transferred my HQ from Nairobi to Kajiado, the base of the Longido Line, and became busy with arrangements for the advance of my division. It meant continual tours up and down the Line, arranging camps, water supply and communications.

I had a rather curious experience to mark the incoming of 1916. On 1st January I, with some of my Staff, went up the Line in two cars. On our way back in the late afternoon we had very heavy rain, and were held up for some time. Then darkness fell, but we had to push on to reach camp. My car was leading and got some way ahead of the second car. I decided to pull up to wait for it, as German patrols were rather active. Suddenly we heard a few shots and as there was no sign or sound of the other car we feared they might have been attacked. After a short wait and to our great relief we saw the light of the car, and as it got close we saw in the back seat the body of a large lioness. She had crossed just in front of the second car. They kept their lights on her and so were able to bag her. Another instance of very non-European warfare!

By the end of 1915 we knew that a considerable force was coming up from South Africa, and that the chief command was to be taken over by General Sir Horace Smith-Dorrien. If the chief command was not to be given to one who had been in East Africa almost from the beginning of operations and had successfully made all the preliminary arrangements, we all welcomed this appointment of a general with a very fine reputation and with considerable knowledge of African warfare. He was bringing with him an enormous staff with very varied qualifications. The Staff arrived all right and had to be fitted in, but Sir Horace himself got no farther than the Cape, where he was laid up for a time and invalided back to England.

We next heard that the command was to be given to a Dutch general. This, I understood, was considered to be a wise political move. All the Dutchmen in East Africa hoped that it would be General Luis Botha, but that was not to be. General Jan Smuts was appointed and duly arrived. Among the Dutchmen he had the reputation of being a very keen and able politician and, as they expressed it, 'very slim', and all knew that he had distinguished himself as a commando leader.

Before his arrival a considerable force had come into British East Africa (BEA), and been allotted to the two divisions. I had several South African units, mounted, artillery and infantry, sent to me. The mounted troops were under the command of General van de Venter, and I took him about with me, showing him the general lie of the land. He seemed most helpful and fell in with all my plans and ideas. The other Dutch officers appeared quite happy in their surroundings, some even expressed a desire to remain under my command, so it was a great surprise when I heard later on that they did not like serving under British officers!

All the purely Dutch elements were transferred to the other division, and I was left with a much reduced command and a very small mounted contingent, though the country and role allotted to my division was much more suited to cavalry action.

CHAPTER XIV

German East Africa – The Attack

The Plan

Briefly, the plan was for the main force under General Smuts himself to advance direct on Moshi, while my force was to execute a turning movement. I pointed out two main points to General Smuts; firstly, that I should be given two clear days' start as my line of advance was longer and more difficult; secondly, if his mounted troops got into Moshi first every precaution should be taken against them firing on my leading units. He asked me when I would be ready to start, and then said that anyhow he would not wait for me and would get off as soon as he could. In the end I started off two days before the fixed date, and when my advanced guard got to Moshi they were fired on by the mounted troops under General van de Venter!

To give you some idea of my ultimate advance I will quote an independent account written by Colonel (later the 2nd Lord) Kitchener, and sent by him to Lord Curzon who was, I think, Foreign Secretary at the time:

> "To move successfully 3000 fighting men, with their attendant artillery and transport impediments, 36 miles through a waterless plain, some 2° from the Equator, and with the probability of being opposed on the march by a well led, well disciplined force of a strength of 1000 or more, required a well thought out scheme by the Staff and troops well disciplined and able to march.
>
> It is well known that the Baluchis, the Punjabis and the KAR would do all that could be asked of them. The Fusiliers had done well at Bukoba, but hard marching under trying conditions, was not supposed to be their 'forte'. The 1st Cape Corps Regiment were all very young and had only undergone some three months of hasty training.

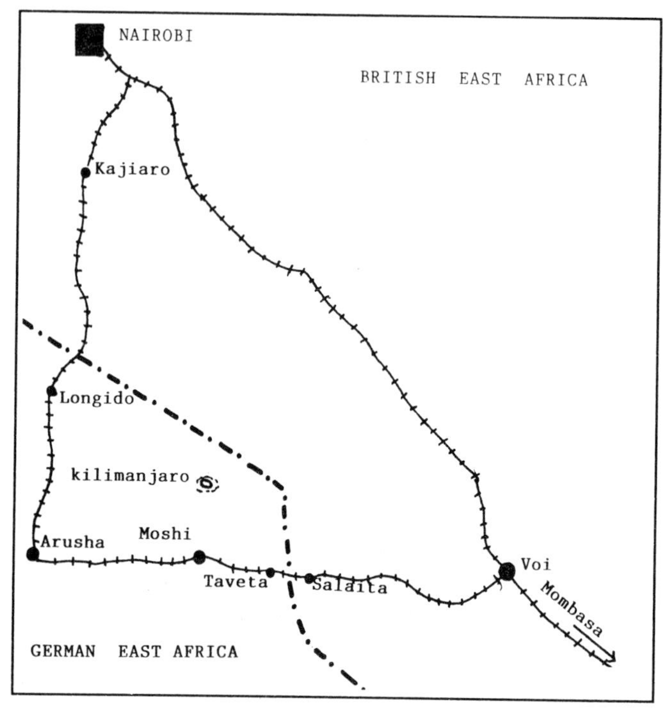

Map 13 — Kilimanjaro and Moshi.

"The infantry brigade, without transport, preceded the Divisional Staff; not a single man fell out, and on the next day only five slight cases, one due to a gunshot wound, reported at hospital. 28 miles, on a dark night over rough country, and every man fit and anxious for a fight at the end of it, is a feat of which any General Officer might be proud.

On 5th March the general situation was as follows:

The main attacking force was roughly 25 miles East of Moshi, opposed by a strongly entrenched position.

General Stewart's Division (1DIV) was roughly 70 miles NW of Moshi with the snow clad Kilimanjaro lying between it and the main force.

The object of General Stewart's small force was two-fold: First, to draw off as many of the enemy as possible from the main position. Second, to threaten his line of retreat.

A fight for the water, with the enemy in a prepared position, was if possible to be avoided, so, notwithstanding its attendant difficulties, a night march was decided on.

There were two main lines of advance; one on Arusha, the other on Ngari Nairobi. Neither of these were taken, though to deceive the enemy the garrison detailed to remain in Longido were sent out on the Arusha road, with instructions to make as much dust as possible.

The selected line of advance was west of the Ngari Nairobi road, avoiding a good deal of bush and terminating in a swamp, where ample water for man and beast was procurable. This line was not direct and covered 36 miles.

On the morning of 5th March our small cavalry force, one squadron of the 17th Cavalry and the EAMR, went forward on the Arusha road. At 0800hrs the infantry brigade moved out 8 miles where, well screened from observation by some low hills, they remained all day. Water had been sent out for them earlier by wagon transport. At 1400hrs the artillery, the ammunition column and both the mule and oxen transport moved off, having well watered their animals first. At 1830hrs the infantry commenced its difficult march, led by a Masai furnished by the Political Agent, Major Browne. The march was, of course, very slow – little more than 2mph could be covered by the men. As it was, in the early dawn of 6th March the head of the column had well passed the kopje on which the enemy's first outpost was placed, before three rockets went up to show that the presence of our force was known. A double company had already been detailed to deal with this party, and a rapid volley almost simultaneous with the rocket signal showed that the enemy were dispersed. As daylight appeared the column found itself advancing over an open plain with bush every here and there, extending some six odd miles to a bright green patch and a line of trees, denoting where the water lay. With hardly any delay the brigade formed for attack; the Punjabis forming the advance, with wide flanking parties on either side. At about half a mile interval came the Baluchis in support, while at a like distance in the rear, came the Mountain Battery, escorted by the Fusiliers. The Cape boys were in the rear with the heavy horse artillery and the transport. At about 0800hrs the possession of the water was assured and the tired troops gladly took up their bivouacs for the night, though not before carefully planned trenches had been dug to ensure their safety.

"At about 1600hrs the tall grass which covered the swamp took fire and caused some anxiety as the conflagration was immense, lasting in fact three days, but the men were full of cheery confidence in themselves and their General, and made light of the troubles of the route.

Fortunately the water was fine and for 2° from the Equator beautifully cool. The cavalry, shorn of its strength by the departure of the South African Brigade for the other front, had advanced along the Arusha road to deceive the enemy as long as daylight lasted. Then they turned to their left and by 0200hrs on 6th March had, without opposition, occupied a range of low lying spurs, covering the right flank of the swamp for which the infantry bde was making. At daylight they pushed on to their left front and occupied without fighting a strong entrenched kopje, which commanded an extensive view of the whole country up to and beyond Ngari Nairobi. They were soon in helio communication with the Divisional Staff. From the kopje in the direction of the Moshi road, extends a plain some 20 miles wide, of a peculiar geological formation. Not a tree to be seen, but at almost every 50–100yds, ridges which look like small extinct volcanoes, as a rule only 3 to 20ft above the level plain, giving the country a very pock-marked appearance. They are covered by short burnt up grass, light brown in colour. On the left of this plain is the snow clad Kilimanjaro; on the right the precipitous Meru – their summits about 40 miles apart.

Of course this country was very favourable for artillery, cavalry and long range infantry fire, so it was not surprising that the enemy should, while clinging to the slopes of Kilimanjaro, retire to where the features of the country were more suitable for their ambush system of warfare. Still, there is little doubt that had not the enemy been surprised, they would have put up a strong fight amongst the bush and swampy country round the precious water.

Fortunately the wind was blowing parallel to the camp and though later on it shifted, it did so in directly the opposite direction, so the work of grass cutting parties was no longer necessary.

"During the march 20 miles of heavy cable was laid, but even though the barrow was pushed out at from 50 to 100ft from the road, it was frequently broken by animals or transport. Notwithstanding, communication was maintained between the Division, Brigade and Longido. After that, it was lost and communication had to depend on the wireless, which took time to erect. A small handy set with 40 miles radius would take no more transport than the heavy wire cables and could be brought into operation in a few minutes. The large wireless set in camp is perfect but a nuisance; its antennae stretching in every direction, and when in use can give the unwary a nasty shock.

On the 7th March a short march took the column to the kopje which had been occupied the night before by the cavalry, and there it halted for the night. Water was obtained from the same stream that fed the swamp. During the afternoon a force commanded by Colonel Hannington went forward and occupied Ngari Nairobi without opposition, capturing a few porters from the enemy's rear guard. There was sniping during the night but no one was hit. 'Horse sickness' – that mysterious disease the origin of which is not yet known, was prevalent here. On horses and mules a slight swelling above the eyes occurs in a few hours under working conditions and in a few days the animal may die. Although every precaution is taken not more than 10% will recover. To avoid losing more animals in this area the Division paraded at 0400hrs and moved 12 miles forward, leaving Ngari Nairobi well to its left. Col. Hannington having detailed the Cape Corps Regiment as garrison, advanced on Ngari Nairobi, while the cavalry moved to the right. About 1000hrs the enemy showed on a well prepared kopje and opened fire. The Mountain Battery shelled their position and as their first shell burst actually in one of their dugouts, it was not long before the enemy streamed off. The river was reached without further fighting. The day was hot and a few men fell out but there were no further casualties. Rations were now getting low. The ration convoys, which were not following the Division but moving direct from Longido to Ngari Nairobi, sent news that the retiring Germans had done much damage to the roads, by cutting trenches across them, felling trees etc. It was therefore decided to halt for the time being and recce parties of infantry and cavalry were sent out.

It had been hoped that by now news of a successful push by the main force to Taveta would have arrived. The only news was that 2 DIV had taken up a position East of Salaita. This information was already known and caused an uneasy feeling. If the main force was held up then the position of 1DIV – already weakened by supplying reinforcements to 2DIV – was now 150 miles from Rail Head and 60 miles inside enemy country. Not very satisfactory!

"Strict orders had been issued not to damage the captured farms and sentries were posted to this effect. Unless the natives stepped in, then should the force have to retire the owners would find their property and livestock as they had left it, though mealies for the animals and vegetables were requisitioned. These orders caused some difference of opinion, especially among some of those who had just arrived from France.

Our guns in action were watched with interest by our Masai followers who with their quaint front and back shields, long spears, and mud plastered hair, looked very picturesque. The firing also attracted the attention of a group of ostrich some distance away, but after the first shot prudence took command and they retired at a graceful trot.

The Germans, evidently having trouble with the insulators used on their telegraph poles replaced them with beer bottles – mainly English in origin!

The country around the north and west of Kilimanjaro is not the promised land the British East African raves about. For the most part it is bare and withered. Where streams come down there are shrubs and – by the help of irrigation trenches – bananas, coffee, mealies and tobacco are grown. The older farm houses are loopholed and arranged for flank defence, showing grimly the terms on which the farmers and the natives lived. Kilimanjaro itself does not improve on closer acquaintance, not looking half so imposing as from either Kajiado or Maktau.

No detail for a night march, however small, can be neglected. The danger of a gap in column diverting troops in the rear has to be guarded against with the utmost care. The telegraph line, if laid by the advance guard is invaluable for maintaining direction. It is necessary that men should be detailed from the heads of units to halt, communicate with the next unit in rear and then join the rear of their own unit.

The lava plains west of Kilimanjaro appear to be inhabited by a burrowing animal who makes his hole like a perpendicular tunnel the size of a large fox earth. Covered by grass these holes are a source of real danger to galloping horses and mules. On the 8th March the whole team of a South African Battery was seen rolling on the ground.

The Masai have a curious way of cooking their meat; they make a small arbour of thick sticks and after covering this with strips of meat they light a fire in the centre. When all falls in the meat is cooked.

That our advance on the morning of the 6th March was quite unknown until the rockets went up is fairly proved, for as soon as they were fired some 50 mounted men galloped from Ngari Nairobi to within 2000yds of the kopje which had been taken by our party.

''Motors are most useful for carrying ammunition, sick etc, and both they and motorcycles travel wonderfully over the veldt. The latter jump about like kittens and the driver, with his feet outstretched to prevent a fall and with his rifle slung on his back, does not look too comfortable. The noise of a motorcycle can sometimes be mistaken for Maxim fire and gives one an unpleasant start.

On the night of the 8th March a loopholed farm outpost, held by a Baluchi piquet was twice attacked, but there was no sniping at the camp.

On the evening of the 9th March the Baluchi column which had been out all day, returned to camp, having burnt a small camp. They brought back as trophies a German flag, German armlets and a few good horns.

The cavalry, who had been searching for water so as to enable the division to move to the right, thereby avoiding the thick bush on the direct Moshi road, returned without finding sufficient water to meet the needs of the division. They had lost one trooper, shot through the head by a mounted German patrol of five men.

The white horses of the German mounted troops have a queer look, being painted with the silver ground from German rupees to make them resemble zebra.

At 0400hrs on 9th March the enemy were driven out of their first position by 2DIV and were pursued by the cavalry to the frontier. So at last, after weary waiting, the whole of BEA was clear of the enemy.

At 0800hrs on 10th March the mule wagons which had been sent back to Ngari Nairobi to assist the ox transport, trotted in with the much wanted four days' supplies.

1DIV was now to be pressed forward, in the faint hope of cutting off the enemy retreat. Unless this could be done the occupation of a narrow strip of country from Tanga to Moshi would be but poor return for the enormous outlay it had entailed. There were therefore two courses open.

First, to move along the Moshi road. This would certainly be met by opposition in prepared positions whilst the Div moved through difficult wooded country.

Second, to go farther to the right across the plain and trust to tracks. Here there would be open country and 1DIV would not be expected. The known tracks were much overgrown, difficult to find and arduous for heavy transport. Also the presence of sufficient water was doubtful.

"Water was known to be plentiful some 20 miles ahead of our position on the second alternative, so that was decided on as the advance route. The infantry started off at midday, having been cautioned to be careful of their water. The mounted troops would move quicker and so they started off at 1600hrs after watering their horses. The column was led by a Dutch scout named Pretorius who formerly had a farm in this district, together with a couple of Browne's Masai.

Moving first in the direction of Arusha it was hoped that that town would be named as the objective. The track wound among the previously mentioned little hills, which on close inspection appeared to have been formed in the past by huge colonies of ants. Low lying flats were passed which held water in places and would, in the rains now nearly due, turn the country into an impassable swamp. A few wild duck were seen, but no other game. As the column advanced the long grass and stones made marching more and more difficult. After about four miles some wood and bush were encountered and a turn was made to the left down a wooded glade. The previously laid telephone wire showed it had been used as a communication route by the Germans between Moshi and outlying farms, but now it was overgrown with bush. It was a down grade however and the DIV pushed on at a faster pace, being sniped at occasionally from the bush on the right. After another four miles the country became more open though still woody. A stream was crossed which had nasty black water the horses did not like and then a halt for the night was ordered. During the night there was a sharp shower and many got wet. 0600hrs next morning (11th March) had been named as the start time but as the cavalry and heavy artillery had not arrived it had to be delayed from hour to hour. As 1DIV was urgently required on the Arusha–Moshi road it was decided to start at 1400hrs, though there was still no news of the missing units, whose absence might be the result of them losing their way or enemy action. There were some 400 men to protect the artillery so there was little to be feared on their account. A double company of 29th Punjabis was sent back to find them.

About two miles after leaving the halt the country opened once again into plains which continued until we met the river at 0700hrs, when a few shots were exchanged with snipers from the left flank. The only excitement was the appearance of a cloud of dust in the far distance which might possibly denote an enemy retirement from Moshi. The troops were glad of a quiet night and the animals were happy to get good water.

In the direction of Moshi – now some 20 miles distant – the sky was lit up by fires. The advantage of choosing the long route of advance was now clear as only for one stretch of four miles on the route had there been any fear of ambush or surprise of any sort. On our left patrols reported enemy movement on the slopes of Kilimanjaro, who would have caused the column casualties and delay had we come through the bush on the main road.

"Apart from the wooded glade where the grass was green and abundant, the character of the country was vile where the column had passed, and viler still in the distance where patches of pure sand were visible. Though Kilimanjaro is close overhead and, from the river the two old craters, called 'Man' and 'Woman' by the natives, can be seen, the view does not give an idea of the grandeur, size and height one expected.

During the night 12 March the KAR captured some natives bringing 140lb of fresh butter for the enemy from the Arusha district, which was duly confiscated for the use of our troops.

In the morning one of our aeroplanes was seen approaching from 2DIV. It circled around us but did not land and as it retired home the Germans could be seen firing at it. Three columns went out early to neighbouring farms, but the remainder of the division remained in camp, hoping for the arrival of the missing column.

About 1700hrs the patrols returned. A few shells cleared the village. On the next river which was four miles nearer Moshi a white flag was hoisted, and the infantry marched in and took possession. The inhabitants were quite communicative, the Germans were releasing the Masai suspects they were holding and were, according to them, getting away from the Moshi railway station. 50 Government tents were found and confiscated, together with a couple of mules. From the wireless news came that 2DIV was making good progress. About midnight communication ceased both with 2DIV and Longido; the latter no doubt due to a move 26 miles to the front to which point permanent telegraph had been completed.

At 0900hrs the mounted troops and artillery began to arrive accompanied by a convoy with four days' rations. It seems that four miles out of the last camp a German company of 200 men who were on the march from Arusha to Moshi came across our line and at once took up a position to hold up what they probably thought was a convoy. The MI of the KAR were on the left, the EAMR in the centre and the 17th Cavalry on the right, with our guns unlimbered in the rear. A determined attack on the left flank with bugles sounding the advance and the German officers shouting to their men was checked about 30yds from the KAR, mainly by shells at close range from the SA battery. After this no determined attempt was made by the enemy to advance – indeed the EAMR pushed forward for a time. Darkness was approaching and the gun position was unsatisfactory. Firing had very much slackened and the order was passed for the concentration of the guns, which had moved to some high ground on their right rear. Up to this time there had been only nine casualties. The sergeant major of the MI had lost his way and had been either killed or wounded. The motor ammunition wagon drivers, who had been mobilised hastily by Capt Giffard to support the KAR, found trouble in manoeuvring their cars through the veldt; all nine of them, were abandoned, though one was recovered later. The motorcyclists were more fortunate. Every machine was brought in. The Germans followed up the concentration, but no more determined attacks were made and the night passed quietly.

Next morning, instead of advancing with their protective 400 rifles, for some unaccountable reason the column returned to the camp they had vacated, followed for a time by the enemy, the total casualties being raised to 13. It appears that the rear guard of the infantry column heard the firing and turned back, but after being fired on and returning the fire it was decided that as it was too dark and they might shoot up their people, they broke off and rejoined the infantry column. About 5000 rounds of ammunition were expended and also 20 shells.

At 0900hrs 13th March the whole division advanced four miles towards Moshi and halted by the river. In the afternoon the artillery with a strong infantry guard retired to the ridge, between the two rivers; the dust they raised in so doing covering the departure of a strong infantry and cavalry force which was detached to cut, by a long night march, the railway about 25 miles from Moshi. 1DIV was now astride the Arusha road in an excellent position to prevent the enemy breaking through in that direction. Having sent forward more than half its strength, and leaving two strong double companies on its line of advance, little more could be expected of it but to stay in its strategic position and await events. During the night 13/14 March unexpected orders were received by wireless to move on Moshi at once. As the infantry brigadier had left, the division consisted mainly of artillery and transport. The infantry was in touch by cable which was laid as they advanced, and so orders were sent for it to change direction towards Moshi. The cavalry having been sent on to cut the railway below Moshi, were unfortunately out of touch.

"The march of 1DIV up to now had been most successful. Here and there along the line lay dead horses and mules, which had succumbed to 'horse sickness', but these losses had been foreseen and provided for. The bush which was infested by tsetse fly now had to be crossed – for campaigning purposes the tsetse fly is not dreaded like 'horse sickness' as an animal bitten will last long enough to get through the work expected of it.

The march went very well; the weather was good and the Germans very unenterprising. Transport arrangements were excellent. General Stewart, by avoiding the upper roads and sticking to the plains disconcerted the enemy and prevented any serious resistance.

On the morning 14th March 1DIV started for Moshi by the upper and more direct route as there was bush everywhere and so the shortest route was selected. After an advance of two miles orders were received to move on Arusha – after an hour's wait the Moshi order was reconfirmed. News came from the advance guard that all bridges were down and the road in bad order – so the lower road was decided on. Here the drifts were very bad but could with difficulty be managed. Five rivers had to be crossed in the 24 miles and progress was very slow, the road being obstructed by felled trees. About 1800hrs the column was still some seven miles from Moshi, with three had rivers yet to cross, besides the one that was then being negotiated – when night and rain fell simultaneously.

In the dark nothing more could be done so everyone had to sit down, wet and dreary and pray for the dawn. What an opportunity for a vigilant enemy! An

Advance Guard, confined by bush to a narrow track; a mtn bty, 3 horse arty btys, an ammunition column and transport galore, spread out for miles; and then the rear guard – what a chance for a de Wett! At early dawn the crossing began again; the SA arty taking the drift in grand style, the Cape boys riding their mules and driving to perfection; at any hitch the battery men with their drag ropes hauling with a will! Then came the transport and all day the crossing continued and not until nightfall was the crossing complete.

At 0100hrs on the 15th March the artillery moved into Moshi; the GOC however, did not move in to the town until the following day. Moshi is not much of a place for a railway terminus. It has a large hotel, 3 or 4 churches, a sawmill and some good shops run mainly by Greeks, a sprinkling of fair residences and all the railway buildings. Up the slopes are numerous coffee shambas.

As the infantry bde advanced with the KAR leading it was fired on by the South Africans. The KAR had six casualties and replied with Maxim fire – things might have been serious but Col. Hannington sent some of his men forward with a Union Jack and restored order.

There should be a hard and fast rule with reference to looting – that every man caught at it should be flogged there and then. Every house in Moshi, whether enemy or neutral, was looted by the South Africans and much wanton destruction occurred. New typewriters were smashed, every locked drawer was forced and their contents scattered. A party of the Royal Fusiliers, finding the railway safe resisted their efforts were found trying to blow it up with dynamite. A Mohammedan gentleman – the happy or unhappy possessor of three wives – came to report that there was a soldier in his house with the latest addition to his harem and had threatened to shoot him if he interfered.

"The night of 15/16th March was like its predecessor, wet only more so. In the morning mule teams and fatigue parties went out to assist in getting the wagons over the deep and now swollen rivers.

It is a wonder, with the lower snow peak of Kilimanjaro just over the town, how hot and steamy it is by day, though it is quite cool by night, which is some comfort. Mosquitoes of the hungriest description infest the place; the drainage is of the worst; the water however is good and abundant.

According to the Greeks, the Germans have a total armed force of 18,000 men, divided into companies of 200 men, each company having from 10 to 25 white men. 6000 were at Moshi, 4000 facing east, 2000 north between Arusha and Kilimanjaro. On learning of the forces advancing against them they decided not to risk a general engagement, but to retire on the Dar-es-Salaam–Tabora line: hence the approach of 1DIV was not seriously opposed, and only a sharp rear guard action took place against 2DIV. Their evacuation began by rail and road on 12th March and was carried out without let or hindrance; the enemy driving stock in front of them. As has been foreseen for some time the enemy has, with little loss of prestige, effected a safe retreat on the Dar-es-Salaam line, adding 6000 men to its defence and leaving in our hands a useless railway and, if we except a few coffee shambas round the mountain, a desolate country. No doubt in a short time the fate of Tanga will be the same as Moshi, but strategically nothing is to be gained by its possession. Between the troops and their main objective, Tabora, lie some 200 miles, 50 of which are desert and the remainder differing very slightly from it. A tram line has been started, but so far the line has been laid for only 30 miles. A start during the next three months is very hazardous owing to the rainy season's arrival. The best thing to be done is what could have been done at first, to restart the war from Dar-es-Salaam."

It was a difficult march and all the troops played up splendidly. 2DIV met with considerable opposition and, I was told by one of their commanders, only carried out their purpose by the determination of their British elements and their British officers. General Smuts, however, without making any enquiries about the difficulties my division had met with and regardless of his previous instructions, told me that he thought our advance had been too slow. Later he added that he was reorganising the whole force into smaller units – commandos – and that there would be no room for senior British generals. We were all to revert to India.

A telegram arrived from India asking that Tighe and I might return to India immediately as our services were required urgently.

So we left Mombasa at once and embarked with General Malleson for Bombay. I was given a great send-off from Moshi by my division; troops lining the road and raising parting cheers.

Before 1914 German possessions overseas included German East Africa, German South West Africa, Togoland and the German Cameroons in west Africa, Kiao Chao on the north east coast of China, German New Guinea north of Australia, and Samoa to the east of Australia in the South Pacific.

We took these 'places in the sun' from the Germans. Just think what trouble we would have had in the Second World War if the Germans had been allowed to keep these possessions!

CHAPTER XV

Aden 1916

On arrival in Bombay on 10APR we were met with orders to proceed at once to Army Headquarters in Simla where further instructions would be waiting for us. We were received there with a good deal of mystery but without any symptoms of urgency. We learnt that Tighe and I had been intended for command of Divisions if threatened trouble on the NWF had materialised. But as the atmosphere had cleared there seemed no particular job for us. Still, we were kept closely tied to AHQ and hardly allowed to leave the vicinity. We hated the professional in-activity, but socially we were very busy – Simla life did not seem much affected by the war. Eventually Tighe was appointed Inspector-General of Volunteers in India, and then to the command of a division in India.

Early in June I was surprised one day by the C-in-C, Sir Beauchamp Duff, an old and very good friend of mine, asking me if I knew Arabic or anything about Arabia. I pleaded complete ignorance, to which he replied, 'You had better begin to study them immediately for you are going to be sent to Aden to command the troops there, and to be in chief political charge.'

I was surprised and by no means pleased, for I had naturally hoped to go to one of the main fronts, and I knew I had been asked for for various appointments. I learned that there had been a good deal of trouble in Aden and that the Turks had established a moral superiority there, both militarily and politically, and that I was expected to restore our prestige.

Soon after learning this news I met an old friend, a head clerk who had worked under me in a headquarters office. He had just returned from France and asked me where I had been and what I was going to do. I told him that I had been in East Africa and was now going to Aden. He replied. 'You must have done something awful in a previous existence for Fate to treat you like this!'

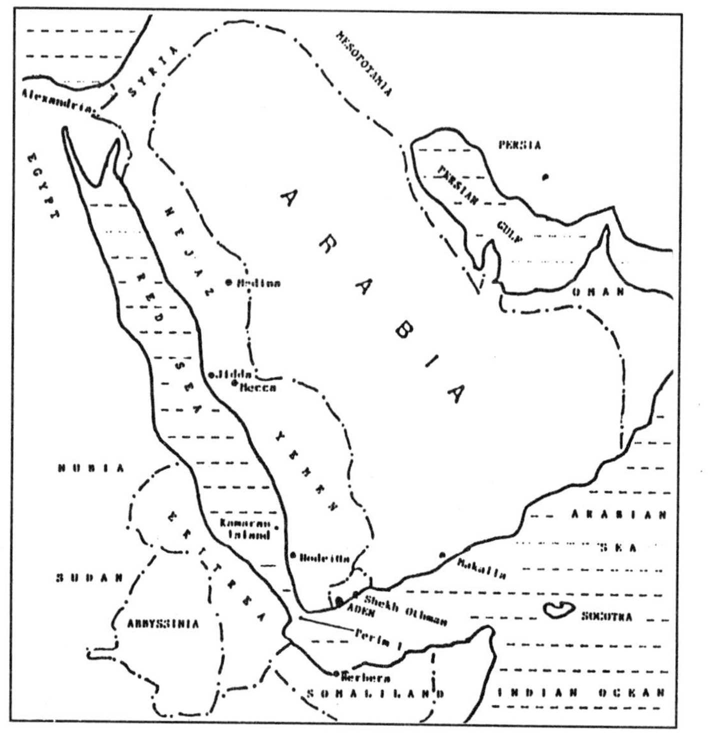

Map 14 — Aden Operations.

I did realise though that I was going to a very independent job, and in many ways rather a big one, for the Aden Protectorate extended well up the Red Sea in one direction and almost to the Persian Gulf in the other. The troops consisted of about one division.

I left Bombay at the beginning of July, and after a very hot and rough voyage landed at Aden on 10JUL. I had passed through Aden many times on my way to and from India but had never landed there; seen from the sea it looked so uninviting and our stay in the harbour was always brief. I had heard that in peace time it was a rather popular station, and I soon found that in war time it had many advantages.

The Residency where I lived was a big rambling building but well suited to the climate which, though hot by day was nothing like so unbearable at night as many stations on the north-west frontier of India. In the house we had electric light and fans and a good ice supply. The troops in Aden itself had quite good barracks, but those in the forward areas were housed in temporary huts, which were very hot by day but cooled down quickly after sunset.

The country itself was really a sandy desert with practically no water supply – the provision of water being our main difficulty. But this shortage meant there were very few mosquitoes and so little malaria. The troops remained healthy and, in spite of their trying conditions, extraordinarily cheerful and animated by a wonderful camaraderie and good feeling, for which I had every reason to be grateful.

The Turkish force was in immediate touch with us and continual skirmishing went on, varied by occasional larger affairs. Neither force was strong enough to eject the other. Their numbers were fairly equal, though to begin with the Turkish artillery was rather superior. In their ranks they had a large proportion of the best class of Turkish soldier and their commander, Said Pasha, was a really capable and efficient officer, possessing great influence with Arabs and Somalis, a considerable number of whom served with the Turks and were very useful in the sandy scrub jungle of our terrain. Several times we captured some of their outposts, but the absence of water made it inadvisable to hold on to them. Gradually we laid a railway from Aden to our forward line, which simplified our supply difficulties considerably; and we improved our road communications with good results. Beyond our outposts it was mainly deep sand which made movements difficult, but it was wonderful how the camel batteries which we organised managed to get about and prove their efficiency.

I realised that our front was a very minor one and that as long as we could hold our own comparatively easily, it was hardly fair to press for reinforcements. Several times I was asked what troops I would require to turn out the Turks; several times I was promised the necessary reinforcements, but always their arrival was interfered with. Those coming from the west were held up in Egypt, those from the east were deflected to Mesopotamia or East Africa, while units from Australia, New Zealand and South Africa were hurried to Europe.

My political work was very interesting, though somewhat strange to me. It involved communication with the tribes of the Hinterland, Somaliland and even Abyssinia, and with Egypt and Mesopotamia. In addition, I had to carry out the duties of an ordinary Civil Governor, the supervision of law courts, treasury, public works, jails, schools etc. I was, generally speaking, very lucky with my Staff on the military, political and civil sides, and with the subordinate staff of Arabs, Indians, Parsees, Goanese, Somalis and others. Gradually, too, my powers were considerably increased. Much larger financial responsibility on both the military and civil sides, and on the military side the bestowal of immediate rewards. In one respect only were they reduced – the death sentence. One of my first duties when I took over was to confirm a death sentence, but later all such sentences in Aden as in other spheres had to be referred to higher authority.

The whole administrative system when I arrived in Aden was strange. On the military side we were under the C-in-C, India; on the political side under the Foreign Office in India; and for purely civil work under the Bombay Government. None of them were in touch with the real war-time local conditions, none of them seemed anxious to help – to be able to say 'no' appeared to be their main object. This system, or want of system, was gradually recognised and a vastly improved arrangement substituted.

On the military side we were put directly under the War Office, and I found them always most understanding and anxious to help as far as the general situation permitted – their desire seemed to be to say 'yes'. On the political side we were placed under the English Foreign Office working through the Egyptian Government and with the Arab Bureau in Cairo. They were naturally much more au fait with and interested in the Arab question. For the purely civil and routine work we remained under Bombay.

The military side in war time was, of course, the dominant one and took up most of my time, but it was the side to which I had been trained and in which my life-long interests centred. But the political work was of almost equal importance and brought me in touch with novel situations, and dealings with French, Italians, American, Japanese and other Consuls and officials.

I had the most cordial relations with our own Navy and the ships working in the Red Sea, the Red Sea Patrol. Their officers were always ready – ready, aye ready – to help in any way they could in small operations, landing parties, etc and all of us welcomed them on shore, where we were able to offer them considerable and, I think, pleasant changes from their cramped and very hot ship-board life, while they brought us fresh and invigorating ideas, and the cheeriest companionship .

One of our small ships had a great success. At nightfall she discovered a German vessel laying mines at the entrance to Aden harbour, and after a stern chase, in which she steamed faster than she had ever steamed before, overtook the enemy boat which its crew sank, evidently with justifiable confidence that they would be rescued.

My life, in some ways monotonous, was varied by all sorts of visitors passing through Aden; Commanders-in-Chief, and senior military and naval officers from India, from Egypt, from Mesopotamia and Africa, and high political officers from Somaliland, Abyssinia and even England.

In the course of my duties I visited Perim, Kamaran, Hodeida, Makalla, Socotra, Berbera, Egypt and Palestine. In Palestine I went round the front just before the final advance, and naturally the dispositions there, and the celebrities I met were all of the greatest interest. Lord Allenby was an old friend of Sandhurst and even pre-Sandhurst days.

In Aden itself I was kept pretty busy with all my varied work. At my own disposal I had a small steamer which enabled me to visit neighbouring ports which were under my jurisdiction; and for getting about the harbour a motor launch which I had originally asked for to check on the smuggling of arms and supplies to the Turks, but which made such a terrific noise that it advertised its movements for miles around.

I visited the front line almost daily and always when active work was going on, either on our own or the Turks initiative. I and my Staff used to leave the Residency in cars well before daylight so as to get by sunrise to our outpost line beyond Shek Othman, where horses awaited us to take us over the sandy tracks. My political and civil work was done mostly in my office, and usually about midday.

One reinforcement we received made our work much easier, the arrival of a kite balloon section and some aeroplanes. As the Turkish commander told me later, that was a heavy handicap for them, for if the planes did no material damage, their morale effect was great, and they were invaluable for observation. At first the Turkish troops were terrified of them, but they soon learned that if they took cover in the scrub jungle and remained stationary, they would escape notice and any harm.

Our planes were often fired on but only one was brought down in the Turkish lines, and Said Pasha immediately sent me word and offered to send in the body of the pilot. In all ways he showed himself to be a most chivalrous gentleman. So when the Armistice came and I summoned him to surrender in accordance with the terms, I was very glad to be able to offer him and his senior staff officers every hospitality I could. All our officers too, naval as well as military, gave him evidence of their appreciation of his conduct. He and his troops were gradually shipped off to Egypt and there reincarcerated.

With the remainder of the Turkish garrison in the Yemen and with the Civil Governor I had much more trouble. They refused to surrender and were supported in their attitude by the Imam Yahia, the Arab ruler, and it was not until I had occupied Hodeida and was able to exert greater pressure that we eventually secured their submission, and were able to report that Turkish rule had definitely come to an end in Southern Arabia. It was a great satisfaction to know that we had held up and finally secured the surrender of over 10,000 first class regular Turkish soldiers. With their departure the Arab and Somali levies were rapidly disbanded and sent to their homes.

I had an amusing incident with Said Pasha. I asked him what he would like done with some of his immediate dependants and more especially with his Somali wife, a lady who I was told wielded considerable influence. I asked him if he wished to take her to Egypt with him. He replied, 'Allah forbid! I only married her for political reasons.' The Mahommedan religion seems to have certain political advantages!

Soon after the Armistice I had a short leave in England and then returned to Aden for the completion of my time. There for three months in the cold season I was joined by my wife and daughter.

After the Armistice, with a view to getting into closer touch with the Arab tribes, I pushed the railway some miles beyond Lahej and posted a strong detachment there; but it proved to be a very malarial district and the men had to be withdrawn. I myself, with a strong cavalry escort, reconnoitred some 60 miles beyond Aden, and was received well everywhere. One chief, to show the honour I had conferred on him by my visit, slaughtered numbers of sheep and cattle, over whose carcasses I had to make my entrance into his palace!

With the departure of the Turks the garrison of Aden was gradually reduced to its normal strength and my own command came to an end. I had a great send off with Navy, Army and civil demonstrations. I realised more than ever how well and loyally I had been supported by all those who had served in Aden and that my appointment there, which I had originally rather resented as hindering my chances of employment elsewhere, had given me wide and, for a soldier, unusual experiences; it had, I hoped, enabled me to do useful work for my country in the Great War.

CHAPTER XVI

With The Red Cross in Greece

I got back to England in June 1920 and, realising that further military employment was practically out of the question, I felt very much at a loose end. I was sounded out by various commercial enterprises but decided that either I was unsuited to them or they were unsuited to me. So we set about trying to find a 'desirable residence' of a permanent nature. This was difficult and so we decided to winter on the Riviera, first at Menton and then in Alassio, but we decided we would be happier at home. In 1921 we established ourselves at Whitchurch in Devon, I took up gardening as a hobby and, against all previous inclination, interested myself in politics as Chairman of the local Conservative Branch.

In January 1923, to my considerable surprise, I got an offer to go to Greece as Chief Commissioner for the Red Cross Society in Greece and the Near East. The work was to organise relief, medical and otherwise, for the Greek refugees who were being expatriated from Asia Minor into Greece. Welcoming active employment and foreseeing that it would be of great interest I accepted readily. I was fortunate enough to persuade Sir Patrick Hehir to come out as my principal medical adviser and the Society, who were most helpful in every way, gave me an efficient staff of English secretaries, doctors and nurses.

We had a most interesting journey across Europe to Greece, and after a short stay in Salonika went on to Athens to get in touch with the general situation and to start to organise our efforts. The Greek Government had already started to tackle the task and the British and American communities had laid the foundations for relief work, but it was a big job for a nation of some five million strong to absorb some one million refugees. They all welcomed us and co-operated heartily.

Our main work was medical and to cope with the threat of typhus and other epidemics. We started in Athens and soon established order out of a certain amount of chaos. The work of the doctors and nurses was admirable and their courage in dealing with typhus etc. was wonderful. They lived in the camps and ran continual risks, but disregarded them. The British staff was augmented by Greeks and Armenians who, under supervision, gave very valuable assistance.

As soon as the work in Athens was in good order I and my personal staff moved up to Salonika and started the organisation of hospitals and camps there in Thrace and Macedonia. We were greatly helped by the arrival of a Red Cross train, which provided living accommodation for myself and staff and enabled us to travel about in considerable comfort, and to avoid the small hotels which were then full of bugs and devoid of sanitation. The Greek Government were most helpful in facilitating all our movements.

For a while the work was hampered by floods which carried away some of the main bridges, but gradually we got camps and hospitals established in Salonika, Drama, Gumaljina and Palazli. A start had already been made by British and American organisations, but there was still much to be done. Our sources of medicine and money were taxed to the full, and we had to engage a large staff to cope with all the enforced increases. We were lucky to find a number of Russian refugees, doctors and most excellent nurses, many of high social standing but all glad to get service and remuneration with us.

I may mention that all our staff on the Red Cross train were Russians. Our cook was a Russian colonel in very poor health and with no culinary experience, but with us he soon became quite robust and, with the aid of a French cookery book, a real chef. The other attendants were ex-Cossack soldiers, most willing and hard working.

Whereas in Athens the main disease was typhus, in Macedonia and Thrace the problem was malaria. But in addition to the medical work in both regions we started relief measures by getting men onto the land, starting carpet and other factories, and helping in the establishment of small commercial enterprises. It was all very absorbing and meant continual travelling and inspecting. But living and travelling in Greece and being able to visit places of supreme historical interest was a wonderful and most enviable experience.

Our system was working most efficiently when, in July, we received orders from the Red Cross in London to close down. They had made every effort to raise funds, but the British public showed little sympathy with the Greeks, and subscriptions ceased to come in. It was indeed sad to leave our work unfinished, but if we felt the closure, it seemed to be felt far more by those with whom we worked. It seemed that we had let them down, but we did leave them a real working organisation, and with a large supply of medicine which we handed over to the Greek Government.

The Greek Government expressed their intense gratitude for all we had done and proposed to give us all Greek decorations but this, for some abstruse reason, was subsequently vetoed by our own Government. This I regretted exceedingly in the case of our nurses. They had incurred severe risks and much hardship and throughout our time had shown the greatest courage, zeal and enterprise.

Sir Patrick Hehir and I were commanded to visit the King and Queen of Greece at their residence at Tatoi, and there received most gracious hospitality and profound thanks for the work of our mission, and sincere regret that it had to end.

On our return journey we travelled by steamer from Piraeus to Venice, touching en route at Corfu and then home by the normal trade route. On our arrival in London we had a very kind reception by the Red Cross authorities, who expressed the greatest satisfaction at the extremely able and extraordinarily economical manner in which our work had been done.

Nothing then remained for me to do but to return to Whitchurch and settle down to the rather humdrum existence of country life and the restriction of 'res angusta domi'. I started the local branch of the British Legion in Whitchurch and carried out occasionally, by request, the inspection of various Territorial units, continued political work and helped or presided over various local functions.

For his old Regiment, the 5th Royal Gurkha Rifles (Frontier Force), we were delighted to maintain touch with him and receive his advice when he fulfilled the duties of colonel of the regiment from 1926 to 1932.

In the Regimental History his record of service after leaving the Regiment is shown below

> August 1914, commanded Force "C", British East Africa; received thanks of Government for successful defence of Colony. Commanded Northern Area on attack on German position of Bukoba, and specially promoted Major-General. Commanded 1st Division in operations against German East Africa. Returned to India on reorganisation of forces in British East Africa and appointed PA and GOC, Aden, where he conducted operations against the Turks throughout the remainder of the war; awarded KCMG and Legion of Honour (Commander). 1920, mentioned in despatches for services in connection with operations in Somaliland. Retired and awarded Distinguished Service Pension. 1923, Appointed Chief Commissioner British Red Cross Society in Greece; received thanks of Greek Government. 1924, awarded KCB.

ANNEXURE "A"

The Egyptian Campaign of 1882

Britain had intervened in Egypt in 1801 to expel the French. The task having been accomplished we had not given much thought to the ruling dynasty of Mohamed Ali which was established in 1806, and was much under French influence. However the situation was altered when the Suez Canal was opened in 1869. This great product of French engineering skill was rendered possible by the friendship between its originator, Ferdinand de Lesseps, and the Pashas Said and Ismail, who supplied the forced labour for the undertaking. In return for this Ismail received a block of 176,602 shares in the canal company. By 1875 Ismail had squandered so much money that these shares were about his only negotiable assets. Disraeli, the British Prime Minister, secretly arranged to buy the shares from Ismail, thereby ensuring that England held a large share in the Canal. England was now in a position to restore her influence in Egypt which had been undermined by the French. It was now inevitable that there would be either rivalry or co-operation between the British and French in Egypt.

By 1878 Ismail's debts amounted to £90 million; the country was being horribly misgoverned and in the following year Britain and France demanded his deposition as "Khedive" (Viceroy) from the Sultan of Turkey. This was acceded to and Ismail's son Tawfik Pasha took over.

Tawfik, a dull but well-meaning ruler, soon found himself in difficulties. The dynasty of Mohamed Ali was in fact Albanian in origin, and almost all the leading officials and officers were non-Egyptians. The native population began to chafe under foreign rule and found its champion in an Egyptian colonel, Arabi. Before long Tawfik was compelled to accept Arabi as his Minister of War, and the virtual ruler of the country.

Arabi's administration was violently nationalistic and therefore anti-foreign. British and French warships arrived off Alexandria but were unable to prevent a massacre of Europeans there on 11th June, in which about 150 lost their lives. This was the critical moment. To maintain her position in Egypt, France must co-operate in suppressing Arabi, but it would seem that a fear of another war with Germany decided the French against locking up an expeditionary force in Egypt. The French warships sailed away and it was the British warships that bombarded the forts at Alexandria and British sailors and marines who landed and occupied the city.

Matters could not be left at that while the Khedive was virtually deposed and Gladstone, now Prime Minister, reluctantly sanctioned a military expedition. Arabi waited before Alexandria with 60,000 men but Wolseley, feinting towards a landing at Aboukir bay, sailed past it by night and next morning his transports entered the Suez Canal. de Lesseps complaining of Britain's perfidy in using his canal for military purposes, was hustled out of the way and the British troops landed at Ismailia, where the freshwater canal from Cairo reaches the Suez Canal.

Realising he had been deceived Arabi took up a position at Tel-el-Kebir, between Ismailia and Cairo, where with 25,000 men he established an excellent defensive position, with a perfect field of fire and with flanks protected by guns and strong redoubts. Wolseley advanced with caution, driving back an Egyptian detachment at Kassassin on 28th August. By 12th September Wolseley's force of some 13,500 infantry and cavalry (including some Indian troops who were on Egyptian soil for the second time) and 60 guns were closed up and within striking distance of the Egyptian entrenchments.

Wolseley now took an unprecedented step. He decided on a large scale long distance approach march and a night attack across the open – and it succeeded to perfection. A naval officer steered the centre of the line by the stars as the force set out after midnight on 13th September – and at daybreak the Egyptian position was surprised and rushed at a cost of little more than 400 casualties. Arabi's army was routed.

By her withdrawal France had abdicated her position in Egypt and control was now in the hands of the British, but the ensuing years were filled with action, with the highlights of Gordon's death at Khartoum and the Kitchener campaign to relieve Khartoum and the final battle of Omdurman in 1898.

For a full account of the 1882 campaign the reader is recommended to read – *The Ashanti Ring* by Leigh Maxwell, ISBN 0–436–27447–7.

ANNEXURE "B"

Black Mountain

When the Punjab Frontier Force raised the 5th Royal Gurkha Rifles (Frontier Force) in 1858 the regiment was located at Abbottabad, with the aim of being able to reinforce quickly any operations on the north-west frontier and to maintain peace in the troubled area of the Black Mountain. The regiment made many visits to the Black Mountain and in the early days could expect an attack from that area. With this fact in mind the Regimental Quarter Guard was located on the North flank of the regimental lines. Until the regiment moved to India in 1948 the Quarter Guard remained on the north face of the lines, away from the main road – which had many advantages!

Chapter III refers to the death of Major Richmond Battye on the Black Mountain in 1891 and the full story of this incident is given in the book *Desperate Encounters*. In this affair Subadar Kishanbir Nagarkoti of the regiment was awarded the Indian Order of Merit – for the fourth time in his distinguished service! It would indeed be churlish not to include his photograph and some details about him in this book.

Subadar Kishanbir Nagarkoti

The first and decisive battle fought by the Kurram Field Force in the 2nd Afghan War was for the capture of the Peiwar Kotal on 1st December 1878. The second phase of the battle was to exploit success to the Shutargardan Pass (11,000ft). This entailed a night advance through the Monghyr Pass, a narrow gorge involving an advance by an ice covered road at night. In this phase the 5th Royal Gurkha Rifles (Frontier Force) were detailed as baggage guard combined with Rear Guard. After five hours of constant close quarter fighting the Rear Guard reached the forward end of the defile, without the loss of one baggage animal. For his outstanding gallantry in this phase Rifleman Kishanbir Nagarkoti was awarded the Indian Order of Merit, 3rd Class.

After a meaningless 'Political Pause', which included the murder of Major Cavagnari and his escort in Kabul the advance continued. In the battle of Charasia (October 6th 1879), which Lord Roberts considered to be the most touch-and-go engagement in his whole career, Naik (corporal) Kishanbir Nagarkoti was admitted to the 2nd Class of the Indian Order of Merit.

On 12th December 1879, during the heavy fighting in defence of our Kabul garrison Naik Kishanbir Nagarkoti was admitted to the 1st Class of the Indian Order of Merit.

Some ten years later (18th June 1888), on the Black Mountain Kishanbir Nagarkoti, now a Subadar (Gurkha Captain), was present at the death of Major Richmond Battye, and for his conspicuous gallantry on this occasion he was awarded the Indian Order of Merit for the fourth time. A suitable award for the Subadar on this occasion posed a problem for the Government of India. Government was not authorised to give him an award higher than the Indian Order of Merit, but he had already won the 3rd, 2nd and 1st class of this order and no consideration had been given to the possibility of anyone winning the IOM four times.

The difficulty was overcome by admitting him to the pay of the First Class of the Order in the rank of Subadar, and by making a special award of a gold bar, to be worn on the ribbon of the Order.

This was a unique award which has never been repeated.

ANNEXURE 'C'

The Subadar Major

The subadar major of a battalion is the equivalent of a regimental sergeant-major in a British battalion but with considerably more duties and responsibilities.

The subadar major (SM) must rise from being a recruit, through all the non-commissioned ranks to become a Viceroy's Commissioned Officer (VCO in an Indian regiment but known as GO or Gurkha Officer in a Gurkha regiment). In 1880 the number of British officers in a regiment was few and the GOs commanded platoons and companies, and sometimes double companies. They were all good – some were brilliant. The SM was the senior Gurkha officer in the battalion. In this appointment he was the commanding officer's adviser on all matters appertaining to the morale of the other ranks, concerning normal military matters and also in dealing with matters outside the manual of Military Law, such as civil offences in maybe the married lines, or soldiers problems back home in their villages in Nepal. In Nepal village law is enacted by a village 'Panchayat', or a council of five elders. In the regiment the SM was the president of this court and under him he detailed four other GOs to sit in judgement on matters coming before them. The verdict and punishment would be made and referred to the commanding officer for approval or otherwise. In this way such problems could be dealt with within the family – the regiment – satisfactorily without referring the matter to a civil court. Such conduct of justice had the merit of keeping a Gurkha out of civil court and ensured that in the case of serious matters the ruling would be in force in Nepal as well as in India, which an Indian civil court judgement could not do.

When away from the regimental home the SM was also the conductor of Gurkha Religious matters, just as the Captain of a ship of the Royal Navy when at sea. In no way would British officers embroil themselves in religious matters, as long as there was no conflict with military discipline and efficiency.

The Indian Army ensured that the least amount of hard cash would circulate in the battalion. The men would be paid out once a month, receiving the amount of money they needed; the remainder being placed in a savings account or a furlo account. Transactions between companies and regimental headquarters and with the Regimental Contractor or Quartermaster were controlled by the Regimental Treasure Chest Officer, who was the SM, poor fellow. He was responsible for drawing pay through the bank and issuing money to companies for paying out. Most transactions within the battalion could be paper transactions, thereby ensuring the minimum of cash and therefore the minimum of temptation. This onerous task fell on the shoulders of the SM and all transactions were entered in his ledger, after which the ledger and vouchers were passed to a British officer for checking. When I undertook this task never once did I find an incorrect entry!

Another important function of the SM was to convene a board to consider the items to be kept for sale in the regimental contractor's shop, their price being compared with that charged in the civil bazaar, and also the quality and cost of items made for the regiment and for individuals by the tailors; also the prices for laundry, haircutting etc.

Take all these administrative tasks and those tasks normally the lot of a regimental sergeant-major and you will realise how important it is for the commanding officer to choose his SM carefully, a bad one is difficult to get rid of and can destroy the morale and efficiency of a unit.

Subadar Major Parsu Khattri was awarded the Indian Order of Merit 3rd Class for gallantry at the Battle of Peiwar Kotal in 1878. In the Tirah Campaign he was awarded the Indian Order of Merit 2nd Class at Thabai in 1897. In February 1900 he retired after these many years of meritorious service with the honorific title of Sardar Bahadur. At that time he had more campaign and gallantry medals than Lord Roberts. He was succeeded by Subadar Jangia Thapa.

'Bullets' Jangia Thapa

Lord Roberts (then a brigadier) commanded the Kurram Field Force in the Second Afghan War which started in 1878. For his close protection he had three orderlies, a Sikh, a Pathan, and a Gurkha named Jangia Thapa. These three orderlies formed a brotherhood sworn at all times to place themselves in the line of enemy fire to ensure the protection of Lord Roberts. To achieve this was no easy task! In those days when modern communications that allow a commander to give his orders from the rear did not exist, a good commander had to be right up in the front line of all engagements!

In one engagement an enemy bullet struck Jangia Thapa on the forehead. The Regimental History states that though the bullet was somewhat flattened Jangia seemed to suffer no distress from the bullet. Thereafter Jangia was always called ''Bullets''!

Jangia's forehead may have been hard but there was a highly intelligent brain behind it and after many years of excellent service he succeeded SM Parbhu Khattri in 1900 as SM. In 1901 he accompanied the Indian Army contingent to Australia to participate in the inauguration of the Australian Commonwealth.

Included here is a photocopy of a painting of Jangia Thapa by F.N. Swinnerton from Lady Robert's Collection, which shows that he must have established with Lord Roberts a friendship based on mutual respect and affection.

INDEX